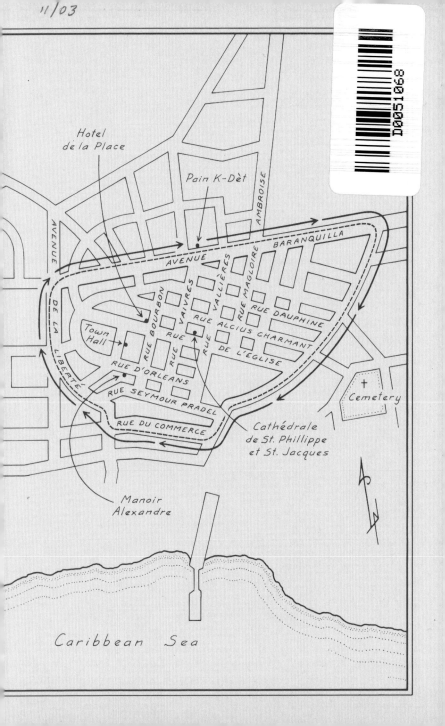

Hotel de la Place

Pain K-Dèt

AVENUE AMBROISE

AVENUE BARANQUILLA

AVENUE DE LA LIBERTÉ

RUE BOURBON

RUE VAIVRES

RUE VALLIÈRES

RUE MAGLOIRE

RUE DAUPHINE

RUE ALCIUS CHARMANT

RUE

RUE

RUE DE L'EGLISE

Town Hall

RUE D'ORLEANS

RUE SEYMOUR PRADEL

RUE DU COMMERCE

Cemetery

Cathédrale de St. Phillippe et St. Jacques

Manoir Alexandre

Caribbean Sea

After the Dance

ALSO IN THE CROWN JOURNEYS SERIES

Land's End, by Michael Cunningham

After the Dance

A WALK THROUGH CARNIVAL
IN JACMEL, HAITI

Edwidge Danticat

 CROWN JOURNEYS

CROWN PUBLISHERS · NEW YORK

꩜ *For Fedo*

Copyright © 2002 by Edwidge Danticat

Published by Crown Journeys, an imprint of Crown Publishers, New York. Member of the Crown Publishing Group, a division of Random House, Inc. www.randomhouse.com

CROWN JOURNEYS and the Crown Journeys colophons are trademarks of Random House, Inc.

Printed in the United States of America

Design by Lauren Dong
Photograph by Leah Gordon
Map by Jackie Aher

Library of Congress Cataloging-in-Publication Data

Danticat, Edwidge.
   After the dance: a walk through carnival in Jacmel, Haiti/by Edwidge Danticat.
   p. cm.
   1. Carnival—Haiti—Jacmel. 2. Jacmel (Haiti)—Social life and customs.
I. Title.
   GT4226.J33 D35 2002
   394.25'097294'56—dc21

                                              2002024165

ISBN 0-609-60908-4

10 9 8 7 6 5 4 3 2 1

First Edition

After the Dance

I took advantage of the break to edge my way into the crowd. The carnival bands had completely taken over every meter of the square. As had previously been announced, the most renowned ones from the South East were there. The musicians and dancers seemed to be camped out for the moment amidst their sleeping instruments: different types of drums, bamboo horns, conch shells, rattles, saxophones, flutes, cones, accordions. Here and there, under the trees, while eating and drinking, the Jacmelians began to tell stories.

RENÉ DEPESTRE,
Hadriana dans tous mes rêves

Jacmel 2001

"CARNIVAL COUNTRY"

*D*URING CARNIVAL JACMEL is not a town or a city. It is a country," Michelet Divers, Jacmel's best-known carnival expert, tells me over a tall glass of lemonade on the airy terrace of the Hotel de la Place, a three-story, white Victorian-style restaurant, bar, souvenir shop, and hotel in the Bel-Air section of Jacmel. The terrace has an eye-level view of a flamboyant-filled piazza, where young men straddle the low colonnaded walls to watch the bustling human and automobile traffic stream by.

I am here for my first national carnival. Since 1992, Divers explains, Jacmel has been hosting two carnivals on consecutive weekends, the national one, which draws people from all over Haiti and the Haitian diaspora, and the local one, which is primarily attended by the residents of Jacmel.

Everyone I have spoken to about my intention to attend the national carnival festivities this coming Sunday has recommended that I first speak to Divers. A stocky

forty-seven-year-old with dark, wide-rimmed glasses,
Divers is a radio commentator and former school principal.
He is quick to point out that he is not the one who came
up with the idea of temporary sovereignty for Jacmel, but
that other Jacmelians would like to see the image of the
southern coastal town of ten thousand, the Riviera of
Haiti, the Ibiza of the Caribbean—as the Haitian tourist
guides say—detached from the one that outsiders have of
the rest of the country, particularly the capital, Port-au-
Prince: dirt-poor, politically troubled, and certainly lack-
ing any celebrations.

"Jacmel is not like that," says Divers, "especially during carnival."

A Jacmelian "by birth and choice," Divers has written
a book about the Jacmel carnivals (*Le Carnaval Jacmelien*)
and this year is the cultural adviser for both. This means
that he, along with other members of the carnival committee, gets to decide which musical bands, costumed
groups, individuals, and animals will be allotted a coveted
spot in Sunday's colorful street parade.

I do not mention it to Divers, but this is the first time
that I will be an active reveler at carnival in Haiti. I am
worried that such an admission would appear strange to
someone for whom carnival is one of life's passions. A
Haitian writer (me)—even one who'd left the country
twenty years before, at age twelve—who has never been
to carnival in her own country? I imagine him asking.
What was that about?

As a child living in Haiti with my Baptist minister

uncle and his wife, while my parents settled in as new immigrants in New York City, I had never been allowed to "join the carnival," as the Haitian-American rapper Wyclef Jean urged many to do in his 1997 *Carnival* album. I was too young (under twelve), small for my age, and we lived in one of the poorest neighborhoods in the capital, coincidentally—and in much contrast to this area of Jacmel—also called Bel-Air. Long pre-Lent days of unbridled dancing, with clammy bodies pressed either against each other or within a few inches of the giant wheels of flatbed trucks serving as floats, were considered not safe for me. However, since I had as intense a desire to join the carnival as some peculiar American children have of joining the circus, my uncle for years spun frightening tales around it to keep me away.

People always hurt themselves during carnival, he said, and it was their fault, for gyrating with so much abandon that they would dislocate their hips and shoulders and lose their voices while singing too loudly. People went deaf, he said, from the clamor of immense speakers blasting live music from the floats to the viewing stands and the surrounding neighborhoods. Not only could one be punched, stabbed, pummeled, or shot during carnival, either by random hotheads or by willful villains who were taking advantage of their anonymity in a crowd of thousands to settle old scores, but young girls could be freely fondled, squeezed like sponges by dirty old, and not so old, men. Or they could be forced to participate in a *maryaj pou dis,* a "ten-cent or ten-minute marriage," that is, acting as if they were wed while simulating sex with a total stranger. And while we were in the realm of dangerous liaisons, there was also the possibility that a person who appeared quite normal and attractive during carnival was not a human being at all, but a demon. Besides, for the first twelve years of my life, Haiti was ruled by the dictatorship of François "Papa Doc" Duvalier and his son Jean-Claude. A military presence at public events was imperative, which made the streets that much more hazardous. At carnival, there were always militiamen and soldiers clubbing people over the head with sticks or rifle butts.

To spare me all this, my uncle would take me and the other residents of his household on a religious retreat in the mountains of Léogâne, the birthplace of my grandparents, where we would spend the carnival week helping relatives feed their livestock and work their land. Some of my relatives in the mountains were also known to sing raunchy songs and tell ribald jokes about wives who temporarily divorced their husbands and abandoned their young children so they could be free to fully enjoy carnival; however, it was my uncle's stories that kept me away from carnival celebrations in Haiti for years.

Even after I thought I had forgotten my uncle's tales, I developed a mild fear of being buried alive in too large a crowd, hyperventilating whenever I felt that a wall of people had grown so dense around me that I would not be able to leave. Later, as an adult in New York, I would faint at demonstrations, having to be carried over people's heads like a heatstroke victim at a rock concert.

After the Dance

Once when I was in Salvador de Bahia, Brazil, a friend talked me into jumping into a crowd of carnival revelers when the crowd was at its most impenetrable, squeezing through a narrow street in the middle of the night. I nearly got my head bashed in by a long line of military policemen who suddenly parted the multitudes with swinging batons and nightsticks in order to force a car through.

That night in Salvador, I had done my best to stay on my feet, which was the advice I had gotten before entering the crowd—drop and people will trample you—and I had landed on a sidewalk not knowing how I had gotten there, but hearing echoes of my uncle's cautionary tales throbbing in my head.

So I avoided carnival, except as a distant observer, watching videotapes sold in Haitian music stores in Brooklyn, weeks after the festivities had ended, and marveling at the revelers' ability to surrender to the sway of so many others, release themselves temporarily from personal and global concerns: the ever present economic and political worries of the country and, in the case of some of the women of Léogâne, the shackles of matrimony and the staunch warnings of fearful relatives who wanted to keep them at home.

Now it was the same fear evoked by my uncle's stories that had drawn me to the carnival festivities in Jacmel. I was aching for a baptism by crowd here, among my own people. I wanted to confront the dual carnival demons, which I had been so carefully taught to fear: the ear-splitting music and the unbridled dancing amid a large group of people, whose inhibitions were sometimes veiled by costumes and masks.

As a child with secret artistic aspirations, I was always drawn to masks. There is an image from ancient Greek theater that I have always liked, a mask with half a laughing face and half a sorrowful one. This mask has always seemed to me a representation of the country where I was born, especially during carnival. Haitians, like the ancient Greek comedians, have always balanced their tragedies with laughter, using distressing situations as the subject of satirical songs and jest. I have also always linked the French expression *jeter le masque,* which means to show one's true colors, to Haitian carnival, imagining carnival as one intense moment during which so many colors are shed that each person walks in the street parade with a rainbow above his or her head.

I was still wearing my own mask of distant observer with Divers, so I didn't tell him any of this. It was only later that I would even learn to verbalize it. Sitting there with him on the Hotel de la Place terrace, I could only think of queries and quizzes for him, questions about Jacmel in general and carnival in particular.

ONLY A FEW feet from Jacmel's city hall and municipal library, the Hotel de la Place serves as a gathering spot for travelers as well as locals. It is one of many such localities around town where people sit on a terrace to talk, have a drink, and watch the street. On the walls inside are pictures of locally known natives, artists, politicians, and writers, the most quoted of which is the moon-faced and bald-headed Professor Jean Claude, who is best known for having written that there are only two great cities in the world: Paris and Jacmel. Around the bar are also photographs of the city before the many storms and fires that have forced it to be modified and rebuilt over the years. The Hotel de la Place, and the terrace where Divers and I are sitting, was once part of a family-run boardinghouse called the Pension Kraft, before it burned down in the 1990s and was rebuilt as a hotel.

Divers chose the Hotel de la Place terrace for our meeting because he's waiting to be called to nearby city hall for a carnival-preparation session.

From the terrace, Divers turns his face to the street to respond to nods and hellos from passersby as he tells me, "In reality, the carnival in Jacmel begins the first Sunday in January and ends on Mardi Gras, the Tuesday before Ash Wednesday. That is officially the length of the carnival season, and during that time, Jacmel is carnival country. Every Sunday during the carnival season, people come out in costume, individually or in groups. However, the national carnival, which you will see on Sunday, is a summary of all of that. Yes, it is a parade, an exposition, but it is also a way for Jacmel to tell its story. Every costume, every mask portrays a part of our story and concerns."

"How many people are you expecting on Sunday?" I ask.

"Last year we had over twenty thousand," he says.

Divers has traveled to Puerto Rico and the Dominican Republic to give lectures and to host presentations and demonstrations of Jacmel's carnival. While he is trying to recall a future date for a conference abroad, he is interrupted by a passerby who wishes to ask him a question.

"Will the mule with the tennis shoes be part of Sunday's parade?" an old man wants to know.

Divers assures the concerned reveler that yes, the mule will indeed be present. There had been a small dispute when the carnival committee and the mayor's office, which gives a stipend to all the carnival acts based on their relative needs, tried to reduce funding for the mule. The owner of the mule protested by saying, "People must think it's easy getting those kid-sized sneakers on four hoofs."

Imagining the labor alone, Divers laughs, he encouraged the carnival committee to keep the mule's funding the same.

Divers cannot speak about what other carnival repeaters will present out on Jacmel's main road, the Baranquilla, in a few days. He is bound to secrecy because part of the fun leading up to Sunday's parade will be guessing what the groups will come up with.

Max Power, the carnival club that was a huge hit last year with a parade of papier-mâché faces of famous world figures, forcing Adolf Hitler to march side by side with Mother Teresa, Albert Einstein, Bob Marley, and Haiti's own deceased dictator François "Papa Doc" Duvalier, has

two spots on the parade roster this year. First Max Power
will repeat last year's performance with the same celebri-
ties, and a few more yet to be named; then the members
will change costumes and return with their pièce de résis-
tance, which is sure to blow everyone away. If Divers
knows what Max Power's magnum opus will be, he is not
telling.

"The carnival must have at least one revelation," he
says, "an element of surprise."

A few more young men have joined the group sitting
on top of the colonnaded walls around the square. The
walls stand in the shadows of *sabliye* trees, whose flowers,
it is said, blossom each day at high noon. People who
leave Haiti and don't call, write, or return are said to have
gone under the *sabliye* tree, for the word *sabliye* with the
last two syllables placed before the first is *bliye sa,* or forget it. In African lore, the *sabliye* is the "forgetting" tree,
which slaves were made to walk under before they were
packed on ships and brought to the so-called New World,
to places like Jacmel.

As Divers greets another passerby, I watch as two
women dressed all in white pace up and down the middle
of the street. One is clutching a Bible to her chest, while
the other wipes sweat from her brow. They are lay preachers exhorting repentance before carnival. Mostly neglected
by the people walking by on their way to the market, or
to pick up a child from school, or to visit someone in
the hospital, or returning home from dropping off lunch
at a loved one's or employer's workplace, the women turn

their attention to the dozen or so middle-aged female vendors whose makeshift stalls pack the sidewalk along the square, displaying everything from candy and cigarettes to soap, perfume, and secondhand clothes. These vendors and their varicolored merchandise often adorn the tourist-pleasing Haitian paintings, which also sometimes take them on as their main subjects.

"Those who love pleasure will always be poor," one of the preachers shouts in a shrill voice, quoting the seventeenth verse from the twenty-first chapter of Proverbs.

As the first one stops to take a breath, the second street evangelist chimes in with a warning from Galatians: "Those who follow the desires of a sinful nature, their lives will produce these evils: sexual immorality, zeal for lustful pleasure, idolatry, participation in demonic activities," and on and on.

There is a level of determination in these clipped, high-pitched voices that reminds me of my uncle preaching the dangers of carnival, an urgency that must have been in Noah's voice as he tried to enroll converts to help build his ark.

Heedless of the preaching, some of the vendors fan their faces with pieces of paper while eating lunches from beautiful silver containers packed one on top of another. Together the containers are called a *sèvis* (service) because they can be used to serve a meal in many courses, as if at a table. Other vendors link hands with the lay preachers and join them in prayer, calling on God to touch the hearts of the carnival-loving hordes and lead them to salvation.

The manager of the Hotel de la Place, Raymond Pascarin, a mocha-colored man with a forceful voice, stops by our table to say hello to Divers. Pascarin and his hotel sponsor a musical act called Relax Band. Relax Band members and their followers will be wearing bright orange T-shirts with RELAX BAND printed in large black letters on the front. Pascarin is wearing one of those T-shirts and a matching hat with his name painted on it.

"Why bright orange?" I ask Pascarin.

"Because it is the colors that make the carnival," he replies.

Divers and Pascarin begin talking carnival. Pascarin is on his way to buy plywood for the flatbed truck that will become Relax Band's float once a portable generator and giant speakers have also been attached. And of course once the musicians have been located.

Pascarin is troubled because some musicians he'd been counting on having on his float have defected to another band. This makes Pascarin angry enough to threaten to suspend the music courses he has been sponsoring for the defecting musicians all year long. In spite of his anger, however, Pascarin's carnival spirit does not waver.

"I have been happy since last October," he says, "thinking of the coming carnival."

That it is now mid-February means that Pascarin has had five solid months of prolonged happiness to prepare him for these last-minute frustrations.

"I couldn't wait," says Pascarin as he departs, "I just could not wait for this Sunday."

A young man has come to fetch Divers. The carnival committee is waiting for him at city hall. Before leaving, Divers explains why many Jacmelians think of Jacmel as more of a country than a city.

"It has its own history, its own literature, its own songs," he says, "all of which you can discover by looking around and by joining the carnival on Sunday."

. . . in the fog of the forests does the migrant bird
nourish itself from the flowering of cemeteries?

RODNEY SAINT-ELOI,
Pierres anonymes

Carnival of the Dead

I HAVE ALWAYS ENJOYED cemeteries. Altars for the living as well as resting places for the dead, they are entryways, I think, to any town or city, the best places to become acquainted with the tastes of the inhabitants, both present and gone.

The cemetery in Jacmel is no different. In fact, it is downright colorful in its vibrant and disorganized mix of old and new architecture, a carnival of stone.

After my meeting with Divers, I ask the poet Rodney Saint-Eloi, who is traveling with me, to accompany me to the Jacmel cemetery. Rodney works for the cultural affairs section of Haiti's oldest daily newspaper, *Le Nouvelliste,* and is the codirector of one of the few publishing houses in Port-au-Prince. Since he has written a long poem that includes a verse about cemeteries, I figure he won't mind coming along. Besides, we have traveled together before and he has always shown a singular reverence for the dead, going as far as dipping his hands in rivers and streams and raising his fingers to his forehead to connect himself to those who have crossed the waters, literally and figuratively, before him. In that way he is a kindred spirit, so I know he will not think it strange if I say hello to the graves, which is something I do now and then when I am in a cemetery.

We head out in midafternoon, when the heat will least interfere with our walk along Avenue Baranquilla, the central road leading out of town. Once we pass the Rue Vaivres and the corner where the carnival's official viewing stand is being built for Sunday, the sidewalk abruptly ends and the large white-and-blue public transportation buses, which are repainted school buses from the United States, double their speed.

The necropolis of Jacmel is off the main road, down a hill with a row of houses on either side. Crossing a wide unpaved road, we reach one of its side walls. A few sections of the wall are decorated with advertisements, one for a cine club where you can sit in a small room and watch a kung fu movie or a Hollywood feature a year or two out of the theaters, the other for a construction-materials store called Kay Dodo. While the cine club's announcement is written in chalk, the Kay Dodo message is painted in red and blue to recall the colors of the Haitian flag. On the walls are also fading campaign posters from the last presidential election, which took place the previous November, images of the recently inaugurated president Jean-Bertrand Aristide, his bespectacled glare fixed on the hills surrounding the cemetery as he appears to be whispering his campaign slogan, *"Lapè nan tèt, lapè nan vant"*—Peace in the head, peace in the belly. The other writing is plain old graffiti, scribbled in chalk rather than spray paint. I find one unerringly appropriate. It is a simple word over a hole in the wall large enough to stick one's head through: BYE.

We enter the cemetery through the back because the wall is missing a stretch there, forming an impromptu rear entrance. Rodney points out that this is a good way to enter a cemetery, for it alerts the dead that we are only on a visit, as they must have learned by now that if one doesn't come through the front gates accompanied by a large entourage, one is probably not there to stay.

There is a saying here: Houses don't have owners, only cemeteries do. In that spirit, this cemetery seems to belong to everyone. Through it runs a well-beaten path, which the neighborhood people use as a shortcut. Teenagers on the way home from school. Young men en route to a soccer game. Strolling lovers. Two girls carrying a *sèvis* of food to a sick relative, rushing because the food is getting cold.

Aside from the area residents, the cemetery has also drawn its share of foreign visitors. The Lonely Planet's guide to the Dominican Republic and Haiti makes a brief mention of it, as does the British writer Ian Thomson in his travelogue *Bonjour Blanc*. Thomson is not at all impressed, noting that the cemetery has "fallen into a ragged state of desuetude. Hibiscus has rooted in the shattered tombs, the lead lettering on monuments bored out of marauding weeds."

As Rodney and I follow the public trail toward the middle of the cemetery, it is hard to avoid these old marble tombs. Many of them are cracked, and rendered anonymous by the dissolution of their markers, some are nearly covered with moss, wild grasses, and weeds, others are reburied under mounds of brown dirt in places where the ground suddenly slopes upward above them.

In 1951, in a public lecture at one of the social clubs of Jacmel, a local resident, the journalist Louis Pélissier Baptiste, bemoaned the disintegration and, in some cases, the disappearance of many of the cemetery's tombstones. "It is regrettable," he is reported to have said, "that the rise of the orange trees and the vandalism of thieves have removed the marble tombstones which would tell us so much about the old city."

To better see the cemetery requires that we zigzag through it, crisscrossing the pebbled soil between the graves. Rodney asks an old woman passing by what the bright green vines with crimson berrylike buds at the foot of the tombs are called. The old woman's knee-length black dress, mourning garb, suggests that she has recently buried a loved one here, or elsewhere. Gently tugging at the short salt-and-pepper plaits framing her wizened face, she looks into the distance, over the uneven rows of old graves and new mausoleums, and speaks in a soft, almost whispery voice.

"*Se flè kouwòn lavyèj*," she says. These are the flowers of the crown of the Virgin Mary.

The Virgin Mary, who does not have the heart to leave her children by themselves in death, gardens their graves to keep them company, she adds. After Jesus was entombed, the Virgin Mary went to the site and wept so much that her tears rained on the ground and created these vines, the green leaves representing her uncontrollable sorrow and the red buds symbolizing Christ's shed blood, the cause of her pain.

And the reason you see the vines sometimes standing at the foot of the graves, she says, sometimes crawling around and over them, sometimes somewhere in between as if kneeling, is because they represent all the physical stages of the Virgin Mary's grief. "And now these same vines grow in all the places where Christ's children, the Virgin Mary's children, are buried."

WE WALK FROM the older graves to the newer mausoleums. Painted in bright yellows, pinks, and blues, they are as elaborate or as simple as the tastes of the owners and their families. Some are built in the shape of houses, with rain drains protruding from the rooftops, steps leading up to the front galleries, an anterior room, as if to receive visitors, and metal grillwork gates and windows with heart- and diamond-shaped designs. The "flowers of the crown of the Virgin Mary" are so high and so symmetrical around some of them that it appears as though the mausoleums have their own gardens. Unlike the older tombs, which were meant for one person, the contemporary mausoleums are family affairs. Rodney points out one that's labeled FAMILLE EDNER TOUTEBON, with only the name of the apparent patriarch painted in red block letters at the pinnacle. The others entombed with Monsieur Toutebon would remain as overshadowed by their progenitor in death as perhaps they had been in life.

Other mausoleums look like small churches, with pitched roofs and steeples topped by a cross. The crosses can be interpreted in many ways: as symbols of Christianity, Christ's crucifixion and death, as with the Virgin Mary vines, but also as representations of the guardian of the cemetery, the *Vodou* divinity Baron Samedi. Baron Samedi, the patron god, or *lwa,* of the cemetery, is honored with Day of the Dead services, held in cemeteries in early November.

During my early childhood in Haiti, the dictator François "Papa Doc" Duvalier would dress like Baron Samedi. Donning a black hat, dark suit, and coattails, he was reminding all Haitians that he literally held the key to the cemeteries and could decide at will who the next inhabitants would be. (A 1963 *Life* magazine article quotes Duvalier as saying, "When they [Haitians] ask me, 'Who is our Mother?' I tell them, 'The Virgin.' But when they ask, 'Who is our Father?' then I must answer, 'No one— you have only me.'")

Along with its religious connections, the Haitian cemetery cross can also be artistic space, representing, as art historian Robert Farris Thompson writes in *Flash of the Spirit,* "the circular motion of human souls."

As we weave our way through the maze of the cemetery, I am reminded of the story of Georges Liautaud, who is the originator of a now very popular form of Haitian flat metal sculpture. Born in Croix-des-Bouquets, a small town fifteen miles or so north of the capital, Liautaud was a blacksmith who carved distinctive wrought-iron wreathlike crosses embellished with heart- and diamond-shaped silhouettes for his local cemetery. Liautaud did not consider himself an artist until his crosses in the cemetery were noticed and admired and he was encouraged to create more of them as objets d'art.

Pauleus Vital, an artist who paints biblical tales such as the judgment of Christ by Pontius Pilate and the beheading of John the Baptist, only staged in the Victorian manors of Jacmel, has set one of his better-known paintings, *Judgement Day,* in what appears to be this cemetery. In the painting, a dark-skinned, long-haired Christ, surrounded by mermaids serving as angels, is floating over Jacmel. Beneath the Christ's feet are the tombs and mausoleums with skeletons leaping out of them.

One of Jacmel's best-known artists, Vital's half brother Préfète Duffaut, has repeatedly painted Jacmel as a city of mountains spiraling toward the sky. In a painting called *Earth, Paradise and Hell,* the dead must pass through an arched doorway with a Liautaud-like cross on top to reach the sky. Once they have crossed this threshold, they turn either right or left, one side leading to Lucifer and a flaming hell in the clouds, the other leading to a paradise guarded by angels with features like those of the Arawak Indians, who were the first inhabitants of the island. The paradise, with its cathedral and narrow streets of ascending steps and cemetery, looks an awful lot like Jacmel. The seventy-eight-year-old Duffaut recently created what some have called his best work: his own coffin, brightly decorated with the real and imagined mountains of Jacmel.

RODNEY AND I are now lost in the cemetery. I notice that there are few trees here. In the mountains of Léogâne, where my great-grandparents and their ancestors are buried, there are no large cemeteries, only family plots, most of which began with one tombstone built under a tree. Over the years when I have returned there, those trees have slowly disappeared, a few of the hundreds of thousands that are chopped down each year to produce timber and charcoal. There are still a few trees left in this cemetery, even though they appear to be on the brink of expiration themselves, leaning sideways as though to give shade to as many of the graves as possible.

We are finally beginning to see our way to the front gates when we happen on a few older mausoleums that we cannot quite categorize. They look like a blend between Mexican redondos and miniature Roman pantheons, with vaulted domes, arched doorways, and folding shutter doors. One of them has its front doors wide open and appears empty inside. Peeking in, I say *"Alo,"* then notice a discarded condom and a pair of torn women's stockings, which seem to have been abandoned after a moment of passion. I walk in farther only to face a dense concrete wall, behind which the real graves reside. Stepping back, I whisper, "Excuse me" and *"Au revoir,"* feeling as though I am one of many who have trespassed on these particular dead in recent days.

Those older, perhaps much frequented mausoleums remind me of a trip I took last summer to the ruby-earthed mountains of Cap Rouge, above Jacmel. Perched on the apex of hills, surrounded by terra-cotta earth and lime-colored foliage, the graves of Cap Rouge are magnificent. Some are like solitary fortresses without any houses near them for miles. Others are in small clusters near very fragile-looking homes that inevitably seem dilapidated by comparison. Others are washed in limestone and gleam so white that in the heat's haze they appear like milky curtains suspended between the mountains and the clouds. One has a tin-roofed canopy erected around it to keep it out of the sun. Another looks like a wedding cake with ascending layers, the newly laid wreaths on the front landing adding to the effect. One particularly expansive one is a series of turquoise-and-white caverns joined together, as in a postlife *lakou,* a communal complex occupied by dozens of members of a very large family.

As Rodney and I exit the cemetery through the front gates, I recite a verse from a poem called "Ton chant est immortel" (Your Song Is Immortal) by Jacmel-born Emmeline Carriès Lemaire, who was a journalist as well as a poet and the general secretary of one of the first feminist organizations in Haiti.

Loosely translated, the verse reads:

> *Look how you are going,*
> *But I am staying*
> *You are taking my soul with you*
> *and I watch over you*
> *I am no more than a shadow*
> *and I tremble*

That evening, Rodney and I make our way to Cyvadier Plage, a hotel near the beach on the outskirts of Jacmel, which has a restaurant on a raised terrace overlooking the bay. More than anything else, I have often come back to the restaurant for this: in the pitch darkness out over the water, every now and then, there is a sudden flash, like an abrupt shower of stars diving in one straight line into the sea. The first time I saw this, I thought it was raining somewhere far away, in the mountains. I was convinced that it was a quiet dry lightning storm, of which we were only witnessing a faint spark, opening and closing the sky before us, with neither the clamor nor the inconvenience of rain.

Rodney thinks he knows where the spark is coming from. It is a spotlight from one of the neighboring islands, he says, a distant electric tower, a passing ship, or the American Coast Guard cruising the Caribbean waters for drug lords and refugees.

But like both the old woman at the cemetery, who told us about the flowers of the crown of the Virgin Mary, and the poet Emmeline Carriès Lemaire, I want to spin my own tale. I think perhaps it is the trembling shadows from the cemeteries, sending us sparkling signals from across the waters.

Indian high chiefs were frolicking freely with young Arawak beauties. . . . Barons and Marquis from the court of Louis XIV were playing leap frog on the grass. . . . In the motley crowd, I also saw Simón Bolívar. . . . The time of masks had assembled three centuries of human history.

RENÉ DEPESTRE,
Hadriana dans tous mes rêves

How Jesus and Simón Bolívar Came to Share a House in Jacmel

THE STORY GOES that when King George III of England asked one of his admirals to describe the island of Hispaniola, of which Haiti now occupies the western third, the admiral crumpled a piece of paper and said, "Sire, this is Hispaniola."

The admiral might have been thinking of many things in making this gesture; however, he was probably trying to duplicate the island's abundance of mountains, which had inspired Hispaniola's original inhabitants, the Arawak Indians, to call it Ayiti, land of the mountains.

A few centuries earlier, another admiral, loyal to another king and queen, Ferdinand and Isabella of Spain, had observed in his log, "This island is very large . . . there are some of the most beautiful plains in the world, almost like the lands of Castille, only better."

The Arawaks who received Columbus and his men were extremely generous with them. "They all came to my men and placed their hands upon my men's heads, which is a sign of great reverence and friendship." According to one of his translators, Robert Fuson, Columbus wrote, "They gave my men bread and fish and whatever they had. The Indians on my ship had told the Indian accompanying the sailors that I wanted a parrot, and he passed the word on to those other Indians. They brought many parrots and required no payment for them." However, even as he was basking in their generosity, Columbus never lost sight of his ultimate goal, that perhaps his hosts, along with their fertile and beautiful land, "might be disposed to serve the Sovereigns."

The Indians' servitude soon followed, and their personal objects and gold, which the Spaniards forced them to mine, left for the coffers of Spain.

According to Eleanor Ingalls Christensen, author of *The Art of Haiti,* "Although Columbus' taste in art may well have been influenced by Boticelli and Leonardo, who were his contemporaries, he was genuinely impressed with certain accomplishments of the Haitian aborigines, particularly their woodwork and weaving. The work of these stone-age people that he brought back with him stimulated the first real interest in anthropology in Europe."

The cost to the Arawaks, however, was great. A hundred years after Columbus's arrival, they had all but disappeared. And the Spaniards, having exhausted the mining possibilities of their lands, moved on to newer adventures, with only a few men remaining behind, primarily on the eastern part of the island. This left a gap for the mostly French pirates who had been roaming around the area. They moved inland and settled in Hispaniola.

After the Dance

After years of fighting between the French settlers in the west and the Spanish settlers in the east, they signed a treaty dividing the island, whereby the section that is now Haiti became a French colony, and the portion that is now the Dominican Republic, a colony of Spain. Slaves were imported from Africa to work on sugar and tobacco plantations, and Haiti became France's richest colony, the brightest jewel of the French crown, as was often said in the 1700s.

Jacmel's history followed a similar course. Before Columbus and his men arrived, it was part of one of the five kingdoms into which the Arawaks had divided the island. Jacmel probably belonged to a southern kingdom called Xaragua, which was run by a high priest, Bohechio, and a high priestess, Anacaona. Of the two, Anacaona remains the better known in contemporary Haiti, having schools and shops named after her. Anacaona has inspired a well-known play by Jacmel-born novelist Jean Metellus, along with countless poems and songs on both sides of the island. Even I wrote an essay about Anacaona, when I met a Haitian girl with that name in Providence, Rhode Island, a toddler whose mother had just left Haiti, fleeing prosecution after an early 1990s coup d'état that unseated then first-time president Jean-Bertrand Aristide.

When I was a girl, I often said that if I had a daughter I would name her Anacaona. Long-haired and copper-skinned, Anacaona was a poet and painter who often entertained her subjects with poetry, songs, and dance. When the Spaniards came, she joined in the battles against them, eventually becoming a casualty to their quest for gold.

The Arawaks would come back to life during the national carnival on Sunday, in the form of children imitating history-book drawings of Arawak dress by dotting their bodies and faces with colored paint and wearing paper crowns over long sisal locks draped over their heads, and by donning shredded skirts hanging from their waists down to their shins. In the style of the Arawak hunters, the children would carry bows and arrows, and without the waist-length mane they could pass for African warriors as well. Some older men in the same body and face paint would carry sisal knapsacks, symbols of the Haitian peasantry, bringing these three stages of history—Arawak, African, and Haitian—together.

Under the reign of Anacaona and Bohechio, Jacmel was called Yaquimel. The fact that many rivers in Hispaniola were called Yaque or Yaqui by the Arawaks indicates that Jacmel was as much a land of fresh waters as of mountains.

When the first French settlers came, it so happened that one of them was named Jacques de Melo, and he gave a variation of his name to the place.

In his public lecture at the Club Union of Jacmel in 1951, which is reprinted in the second volume of Jean-Elie Gilles's two-part work *Jacmel, sa contribution à l'histoire d'Haiti* (Jacmel: Its Contribution to Haitian History), the Haitian journalist Louis Pélissier Baptiste recalls that the first street in Jacmel was a narrow gorge located between two cactus-covered hills.

For a long time, Jacmel's European settlers, who specialized in tobacco production, were afraid to build brick or concrete houses. Living between two cliffs, they feared the crushing consequences of earthquakes. A century after the town was founded in 1698, of the forty houses erected on the main street, only one was built in brick, and the owner was thought to be insane.

Stifled by the twin hills, Main Street was unbearably hot in those days, and during the rainy season, mosquitoes swarmed around the rivers. To find relief from the heat, the mosquitoes, and the resulting cases of malaria, the settlers flattened out the cliffs and expanded Main Street. Of the two, now smoother elevations, one became the site of a hospital and the other became the Bel-Air section of town. The older neighborhood, which was closer to the port, became the commercial center, with the main thoroughfare being Rue du Commerce, or Commerce Street.

Forced to sell their tobacco at less than competitive figures because of mainland France's price-fixing, Jacmel's land-owning class searched for more profitable crops. Coffee was perfect for the mountainous landscape, and soon Jacmel became a hub of coffee production and export. Wealth from coffee led to the expansion of the town. Everyone benefited except the slaves, whose blood, as Voltaire might have exclaimed, filled every cup of coffee in France.

In the carnival this coming Sunday, there will also be a group of armed men dressed as white colonists, commanding black slaves hauling heavy logs along the parade route.

The men portraying the colonists will wear Caucasian flesh–colored masks and cloche-shaped sun hats with the words COLON BLANC printed on the front. The colonists will don spotless white shirts and breeches, an effect created by raising white socks over the lower ends of long dark pants, to contrast with the slaves' bare torsos and tattered trunks. The slaves will wear dark sacks over their faces, with holes only for their eyes and mouths. One slave will be crouched inside a small hut no larger than a dog kennel. He will crawl along the ground on his knees as he carries the hut with him and tries to avoid the wrath of the master, who, when the slaves pause to rest, shoves them along with kicks or the butts of rifles.

Even on a parade route, with music blaring and people dancing and laughing, this festive reconstruction still gives one pause. According to Peter Mason, a chronicler of Trinidad's renowned carnival, "In Roman times, carnival took the wild form of Saturnalia, when slaves were freed for seven days of drunkenness and allowed, theoretically at least, to exchange roles and clothes with their masters." The slaves of Haiti would not have been appeased by mere role reversals. They wanted the real thing, poisoning their masters whenever they could and setting their plantations on fire. For this they suffered, getting their heads cut off and hung on pikes along the roads leading to the plantations, as an example for the others.

With their profits from the coffee boon, the colonists sent their offspring, the children they sired with their slaves and free blacks, to study in Europe. When these educated children returned to the island, they too became the owners of property and slaves, joining a class of free blacks and mulattos called *affranchis*.

Though they had the same land-ownership rights as the whites, the *affranchis* were not allowed to wear the same clothes, or sit in the same public places, and when they revolted, they were publicly executed.

There is an old military fort in the mountains of Cap Rouge called Fort Ogé. Built in 1804, on the orders of the revolutionary leader Jean-Jacques Dessalines, the fort was erected to honor Vincent Ogé, one of the first to bring his case for equal rights for *affranchis* to the General Assembly in France. When he returned to the island, Ogé was arrested. All his limbs were broken with metal bars, and he was placed on a giant wheel and left to die.

Ogé's fort is now only a shell of what it once must have been. At the entrance to its open courtyard, two old cannons are slowly sinking into the ground, looking as if they are likely to disappear altogether under the thump of the next heavy rain. In the courtyard, where the children in the area have chalked markers and planted bamboo goalposts for a soccer field, a few colorful butterflies glide over the heads of the goats tied to graze on plants growing out of the cracks in the stone walls.

From the fort's upper level, I see the bay of Jacmel, the port, the sea. On the farthest tip toward the gulf, there is a watchtower with a narrow entrance. It is relatively free of vegetation, so the occasional visitor carves his or her name there, making a guest book for the ages.

When I come down on another side of the wall, I land in a cornfield. Near the cornfield is another entrance to the fort, a dark cavelike root cellar with moss-filled interiors that seems to go on forever.

"This room can take you anywhere in Haiti," a future soccer star tells me.

"Has anyone ever disappeared in here?" I ask.

"No," he replies sternly. "Sensible people know not to go inside."

DURING THEIR BATTLES with the French, the Spanish, and the British, all of whom wanted to conquer the colony, the slaves had their own leaders and the *affranchis* had theirs. The slaves had, among others, Toussaint-Louverture ("Few people have ever received more extravagant adulation," Alec Waugh wrote in *Love and the Caribbean*), and two of the *affranchis'* leaders were General Alexandre Pétion, who would later become president, and Pierre Pinchinat, who has a secondary school in Jacmel named after him.

At times, the slaves found themselves fighting against both the foreign powers and against the *affranchis*. In the end, however, slaves and *affranchis* united to fight the battle for independence that led to Haiti becoming a free republic in 1804.

In postindependence Haiti, General Pétion became president of the southern region, including Jacmel.

Inspired by the Haitians' fight for independence, the Latin American revolutionary Simón Bolívar stopped in Haiti on his way to Venezuela to free it from Spanish rule. Bolívar's send-off by General Pétion is described in dramatic form by one of his biographers, Nina Brown Baker, in *He Wouldn't Be King: The Story of Simón Bolívar.*

> *"And now, sir . . ." He [Bolívar] held out his hand. "It is good-by. I have no words to express the gratitude which fills my heart. If only there were some way in which I could hope to repay your kindness!"*
>
> *The older man [Pétion] grasped the extended hand. "There is a way, my son, but I will not urge it upon you. You sail in the name of freedom. Have you reflected that there are men in your land who have never dared hope for that blessing? Yet the love of liberty works as strongly in the breast of the black man as in that of the white. If—"*
>
> *"You need say no more!" Bolívar interrupted him. "We Americans know too well the bitterness of slavery, for we have endured nothing less from our Spanish masters. Do not ask my promise as a reward, but allow me to offer it as a duty and a privilege. Your Excellency, I give you that solemn promise now, upon my word as a gentleman and a patriot. My first act upon reaching my native land shall be to proclaim the abolition of slavery!"*

Upon returning to Venezuela, Bolívar abolished slavery; however, in doing so he alienated much of his support base. He returned to Jacmel, where he stayed six months in a corner house overlooking the current iron market, a few steps from Saint Phillipe and Saint Jacques Cathedral.

In accounts of older carnivals, there are reports of men wearing Bolívar hats. The novelist René Depestre describes these hats as being made with multicolored papier-mâché, bright feathers, and long locks of hair. This; the main street, the Baranquilla, which is named after a Colombian city; and the Place Simón Bolívar, near the port, are three of the most memorable reminders of Bolívar's stay in Jacmel.

I understood the depth of Bolívar's gratitude to Haiti and General Pétion only when I visited the house where he spent his later years, in Bogotá, Colombia. At the gate is a bust of Pétion, one of the first sights to welcome visitors.

The house where Bolívar spent his days in Jacmel, however, is much less conspicuous for its historical purpose than its present one. Bordered with white iron gates, it is a bright pink two-level building lodging a shop that sells dresses and school bags, a place called the Merci Jesus Shop. In a corner high above the doors is a simple marble plaque that reads ICI A RESIDÉ SIMON BOLÍVAR EN 1816 (Here resided Simon Bolívar in 1816).

The visit to the Bolívar house echoed another visit I had tried to make to a location linked to the Haitian war of independence. On the site of a current Catholic school is La Petite Batterie, a small gathering of cannons that were used during the battles for independence. A friend in town offered to take me to see the cannons. When we arrived at the school, we were met at the gates by one of the priests. We could not enter the private property, he said. Since someone had written about them in a guidebook, he was being overwhelmed by the number of people who were coming by asking to see the cannons.

The cannons were going to be moved to another location, he said, somewhere up in the hills.

"Won't they lose their context?" my friend asked.

"No," the priest replied. "They will still be the same cannons. That will never change."

Simón Bolívar's house is a dress shop. Ogé's fort is a soccer field. Anacaona is living in Providence, Rhode Island. History is moving on.

It is no great sea that sunders him from me,

no endless road, no mountain peak, no town's

high walls with gates shut tight: no, we are kept

apart by nothing but the thinnest stretch

of water.

OVID,
Metamorphoses

Ovid's Jacmel

*R*ODNEY AND I are looking for a symbol of nineteenth-century industrial Jacmel when we find ourselves completely lost. Our destination is an abandoned steam engine scattered in two very large pieces across a grassy plain that was once the site of a thriving sugar plantation called Habitation Price.

We walk in and out of several banana fields, past some brightly painted one-room peasant houses, through a few yards and gardens, and still find no visible signs of this engine, which we had expected to be as conspicuous as a palm tree on Mars.

I had visited the rusting Habitation Price steam engine some years before, with a group of college students on a trip sponsored by the Ministry of Haitians Living Abroad. Our guide on that first visit, a woman from the Ministry of Tourism, had told us that the steam engine was one of a handful of Watt engines left in the world. Among the first patented by the Scottish engineer James Watt, it was brought to Haiti in the early 1800s by a former British military man named Price. The Habitation Price steam engine is such a valuable relic that the Smithsonian archeological society is said to have offered to remove it from its outdoor location in Jacmel to one of its museums in the United States. It was with this engine that the industrial revolution had made its way to Jacmel.

Now, as I walk past a group of men working a furrowed field with pickaxes and hoes, it seems to me, as it did during my previous visit, that if the industrial revolution had come to this area, it had only stopped by to visit and had not come to stay. Peasants were still going about their lives and working their land just as they had hundreds of years before. But then steam engines and their like were never meant to ease the working lives of peasants anyway. They were purchased and brought to places like this to increase profits for their owners.

WE ARE ON the verge of abandoning our search for the steam engine when we run into Ovid. Haitians with Roman names are not that uncommon; however, this is the first Haitian Ovid I have ever met.

Ovid emerges from a banana field with a machete in his hand and sweetly asks us what we are looking for.

I reply, "Habitation Price."

"Se isit la," he says, clearing his throat. "It is here." The whole area is called Habitation Price.

At one point the entire commune might have been part of the Price sugar plantation.

"We are looking for the old engine," I say.

Ovid is wearing a blue shirt with the word HAWAII printed on the front. The shirt has seen better days. He takes a moment to apologize for the state of the shirt. Though he obviously knows where the engine is located, Ovid does not offer to tell us or to show it to us immediately. Instead he decides to share the story of his life.

Ovid was born in Jacmel in 1946. At that time a man named Dumarsais Estimé was president. The year Ovid turned three, Estimé presided over lavish celebrations of the bicentennial of the capital, Port-au-Prince, which Ovid could not attend because he was too young.

Ovid's parents were peasant farmers who produced bananas, mostly. And even now, there are enough banana trees around Ovid's one-room pink-and-green house to dress a whole troupe of a carnival group called Fèy Bannann, who are people covered from head to toe with dried banana leaves. (According to Divers, the Fèy Bannann disguise was introduced to the Jacmel carnival by children of the bourgeoisie who had traveled to Germany and had come across the straw-clad, bell-ringing figure of Knecht Ruprecht, who during the season of Advent walks through small villages rewarding children who can recite their prayers and punishing those who cannot. Since dried banana leaves were more readily available in Jacmel, they replaced the German straw in the local variation of the costume.)

As far as he can recall, Ovid has always lived in the area called Habitation Price. With the defunct engine never too far away, he began farming as a boy. Now a tautly fit man with bulging muscles in his arms and chest, he has never been to school. His parents didn't have enough money to send him, and they needed him at home to help them work the land.

"Life has always had no guarantees," Ovid says. There were few days in the year when his parents were not worried about the crops, their pigs, chickens, and goats, and their children, who were always in danger of getting sick and dying.

When Ovid was old enough, he built his own house and took a wife. They had four children; then his wife died. His new wife is younger than he is. She too had a husband and children before she and Ovid moved in together. Ovid's children are in Port-au-Prince now, working in the capital. He has three nieces living in the United States. When things are difficult for him financially, he does not like to ask his children or his nieces for money, even though he knows they would be happy to send him some.

"If I ask and they give me today," he says, "one day I would like to give them too."

Right now, Ovid feels he has nothing to give. He suffers from a back problem, which prevents him from pulling a few coconuts off his tree to offer his visitors some coconut water.

"This is not very hospitable," he says.

Finally Ovid's thoughts shift to the dozen or so people he has seen walking by each week on their way to visit the remnants of the old steam engine.

He would like to see more people come, he says—hundreds, maybe thousands. A better road would help. The path now leading to his home and the engine, he says, is a dirt road that becomes impassable when it rains.

"If we had a good road then more people would come to see the engine and the area would benefit," he says.

Ovid would also like to see electricity come to his part of Jacmel. His house is only a mile or two off the main road; however, electric poles and cables have bypassed him. Even though Jacmel was one of the first places in Haiti to have electricity, Ovid has never benefited.

"We still use lamps at night," he says. "Why?"

People like Ovid, rural people, who make up the majority of the country's population, are still part of what is called the outside country, the *peyi andeyò*. They are often subsistence farmers working small plots of land, which might belong to them, as in Ovid's case, or might belong to big landowners, to whom they owe a large share of what they produce. To send their children to school, build a house, or bury a loved one, they raise a farm animal, a cow, a goat, or a pig—until recently, when the United States Food and Drug Administration ordered 99 percent of the population of Haitian Creole pigs exterminated, claiming they were infected with swine fever. People like Ovid are mocked in comic television or theater programs, which poke fun at their lack of comfort or familiarity with urban settings, or they are revered in folk-loric dances when people dress up in what was once their daily garb of bright blue denim dresses or pants and red scarves or madrases. Still, they are like Maroons in their own country, excluded from any national decision-making process, remaining symbols more than anything else of the bread basket of a country that increasingly looks for its bread abroad, valuing imported foods above those produced at home.

When they move to the cities, they live in *bidonvilles,* popular neighborhoods, which I always refrain from calling slums because I have lived in one. And whenever people call these poor neighborhoods slums, I remember a quote from Langston Hughes that says something like misery is living in a place that everyone calls a slum but you call home. However, many of the people who have left their land to live in these neighborhoods have done so mostly to give their children a better life, to spare them the whims of the gods of rain and no rain, the unpredictability of Mother Earth. In the city, they feel that their children will have better opportunities for schooling, either at a public school or one of the many privately run schools that crowd the capital.

Ovid's tale and his forward way of telling it captivate me because I come from this stock of people. F. Scott Fitzgerald once said that there is a peasant in every novel-ist; in my case this is doubly true. Ovid could be one of my relatives. My grandfather was a man just like him, a peasant farmer who sent his sons and daughters to school and stayed behind in the mountains of Léogâne until the land where he grew his coffee, beans, plantains, and corn became too unreliable. This forced him to move to that other Bel-Air, where my family's urban roots first sprang.

WHEN OVID IS tired of talking, he takes us home to meet his wife, who identifies herself simply as Madame Ovid. Madame Ovid is a slender woman with a long face and high prominent cheekbones. Her hair is pulled back in a tight bun, with gray roots at the temple.

After she greets us, Madame Ovid returns to where she was sitting under the extended leaves of a banana tree, gluing pieces of brown paper into small cones, which she will fill with grilled corn flour to sell in town during carnival. Usually she sells by the main road in the afternoon, but she will take advantage of the larger crowd in town this weekend to earn a few extra gourdes. Madame Ovid is much more reserved than her husband. Her eyes never wander far from her working hands as she carefully chooses the few words that she utters.

In her size and carriage, she reminds me of my aunt Ilyana, who died in the mountains of Léogâne last year. Aunt Ilyana was the last close family member still living in the mountains. Everyone else had migrated, first to the capital and then to other parts of the world.

Nestled between a stream and a banana grove, my aunt Ilyana's two-room home was made of limestone walls and a tin roof, which had been replaced a couple of times due to hurricanes. Aunt Ilyana lived alone, even though her ex-husband had his own place nearby and visited often, as did her adult son, my cousin Renel, who is a dentist in Port-au-Prince.

When Aunt Ilyana died, at seventy-six years old, our grief was compounded by logistical frustration. It had taken a day for news of the death to travel to Port-au-Prince and then by telephone to us in New York, which meant that Aunt Ilyana's funeral had already been held. Attending the burial was not even an option. There are no morgues in the mountains of Léogâne. The body could not wait, so none of us got to say good-bye. But I feel as if I am seeing Aunt Ilyana all over again in Madame Ovid, and relatives long gone in Ovid himself.

Rodney and I spend most of the afternoon with them, listening to their stories but mostly their complaints: about the lack of opportunities, the bad roads, the need for a widespread irrigation system to water their crops.

"The land is furious," Ovid says. "We are poor. We would like to help our country, but we need help first. If there is no peasant, there is no country. When you wake up in the morning and the land stares at you like the white balls of your eyes, what are you supposed to do, stare back at it all day long?"

The more Ovid talks, the more I realize that in every peasant, there might also be a proletarian novelist.

Toward the end of the conversation, Ovid turns to carnival. He tells us that he will not go to the carnival.

Not because he wouldn't enjoy it, but because he has a bad back and cannot walk too long. His wife will go, to sell her wares, but she will also enjoy watching all the costumes and the groups going by.

Ovid will listen to the carnival on the radio, imagining the colors and the crowds in his mind. He is proud of Jacmel's carnival, he says: "It is the best carnival in Haiti."

Ovid points in the direction of the steam engine as we say good-bye. When we happen on the site, at first I am startled by the donkey tied by a sisal rope to what seems like the base frame, firmly anchored in the brown soil. The flywheel is some ways off in the distance, near a harvested cornfield. Still standing upright, the wheel looks like a small shipwreck, part of some strange vessel that has washed ashore.

During that first visit, these two large chunks had seemed almost grand to me, constant and durable in spite of the century-old layers of rust covering them. I had thought of them as symbols of Haiti—I was always looking for such symbols—weathered and depreciated, but still robust and stalwart at the core.

At that time, I had tried to imagine the stories that the engine might tell, if only it could, two centuries' worth of tales about the changes, or lack of changes, in the natural and human landscapes.

This time, however, I am thinking that perhaps the "beauty" of this engine lies in the tales that it does not tell. The fact that there are no signs indicating its locale, no cards explaining its importance, no admission fee for the privilege of gawking at it forces its rusty fragments to be its only testimony.

I prefer looking at it this way, without a guide encouraging me to admire or appreciate it. I like the blank slate, the silence, which allows for ambiguity. I can love it, despise it, be indifferent to it, or all three. There is neither forced celebration nor a condemnation in the moment. It is simply a flash of an era frozen in time.

I was also one of the carnival masks.

RENÉ DEPESTRE,
Hadriana dans tous mes rêves

Hadriana in Jacmel's Dreams

J ACMEL'S RESIDENT GODDESS is Hadriana Siloe. One of the most beautiful women in town, Hadriana dies at the altar in the middle of her wedding ceremony. Her body is exposed at the square for a public wake before her funeral. Except she is not dead. It only appears so. Her apparent demise was caused by a man with mystical powers who shows himself as a giant butterfly. Hadriana becomes a zombie.

A few hours after her burial, Hadriana is exhumed from her grave but manages to escape, running off to the mountains, where she is mistaken for Simbi Lasous, the spirit of springs and fresh waters, and is invited to accompany a group of migrants off to permanent exile in Jamaica.

This is the premise of René Depestre's *Hadriana dans tous mes rêves* (Hadriana in All My Dreams), a celebrated novel set in Jacmel. Born in Jacmel in 1926, the poet–novelist Depestre is one of Haiti's most prolific and best-known writers. The winner of several prestigious international prizes, he is considered by some to be Haiti's best shot at a Nobel Prize. Even though he has been living outside of Haiti for more than forty years and has never returned, Depestre draws upon childhood memories of the 1938 carnival season for his 1988 novel, and in it he has created a character that lives far beyond the pages of his book.

Hadriana is one of those rare literary cases in which a novel's character becomes even more real, and more powerful, than actual people. For many Jacmelians, including Divers, even pondering her existence parallels the question that many agnostics ask themselves about God. Did we create God or did God create us? Did Depestre and Jacmel create Hadriana or did she create Jacmel and Depestre?

"Hadriana's death so shakes the foundations of the city," writes literary critic Sílvío Torres-Saíllant in his book *Caribbean Poetics,* "that over thirty years after the event the narrator can establish a link between Hadriana's departure and Jacmel's socioeconomic decline."

Depestre's novel has such influence that pieces of it seem to appear everywhere. The national Haitian tourist guide borrows from the title of the book for the heading of its section about Jacmel: "Jacmel in All Your Dreams." The international guides often list the striking white-and-green Hotel Manoir Alexandra, a towering presence perched between the upper and lower levels of the city, as the home of Depestre's famous character, which, as the novel-fed legend has it, was once called Manoir Hadriana. The French

tourist guide *Le Petit Futé* claims that "this beautiful building can be ranked in the category of haunted hotels or to
use the local lingo, zombie hotels." While visiting Jacmel,
the novelist Tracy Chevalier decided to stay at the Manoir
Alexandra mostly because of the book. She is not the only
one. Over the years, many visitors have come to Jacmel,
novel in hand, looking for Hadriana.

Hadriana's lore has strong connections to the carnival
as well. Because Hadriana's death takes place during carnival season, the novel offers firsthand descriptions of
perennial carnival figures, two of the most memorable
being the *chaloska* and the zombie.

The *chaloska,* a character in military garb with a protruding mouth and clawlike teeth, is based on an actual
military officer, Charles Oscar Etienne, who terrorized
Jacmel in the early 1900s with group imprisonment, summary executions, and arson, destroying entire neighborhoods. By Depestre's account, the old *chaloska* bands, which
were formed to caricature and playfully protest military
abuse, carried signs on their backs that read COLONEL, IT
GETS WORSE LATER ON, COMMANDER OF HOUSEHOLD TRIBU-
LATIONS, and GENERAL OF DAMNED VINDICTIVE RODS. There
would be no signs on the back of the *chaloskas* I would see
on Sunday; however, signs are not necessary. Everyone
knows who they are.

As a child, there were moments when even though I
didn't go to the carnival, it came to me. Every Sunday
afternoon during carnival season, a band of *chaloskas* would
stop by our house, crack their whips, and growl at us from

the street. Upon spotting them, I would quickly run and hide, far enough away that the *chaloskas* wouldn't catch me, but never too far that I wouldn't be able to safely observe them.

For some reason, the *chaloskas* focus particularly on children, who can either run away from them or confront them with a simple rhyme, which is supposed to make the *chaloskas* go away:

> *Chaloska m pa pè w;*
> *Se moun ou ye.*
> *(Chaloska, I'm not afraid of you;*
> *You're a human being.)*

From my secure hiding place, I would sing this rhyme, never venturing close enough for the *chaloska* to hear my quivering voice.

Chaloska, I'm not afraid of you; / You're a human being.

A human being as opposed to what? I was not sure then. But when I think of it now, I guess this was a way of demilitarizing, defanging a monster, making him ordinary.

In the carnival on Sunday, I would say this rhyme with no fear for the very first time, as the *chaloskas* would stroll by me, ignoring me to chase the children, many of whom, raised on television and movie monsters, would laugh as they recited the rhyme, as if following Plutarch's exhortation that the only way to subdue a fear of masks is to bring the mask close and uncover its hollowness and "theatrical imposture."

In the carnival on Sunday, I would also see a zombie, one with a white sheet covering its face and body, and heavy chains wrapped around its shoulders, chest, and waist. I would remember how Depestre in a 1997 interview with a Canadian journalist had explained why he had never returned to Jacmel after having left Haiti in 1959, during the reign of the dictator François "Papa Doc" Duvalier. Instead he had set up residence in eastern Europe, Russia, Cuba, and finally the South of France.

"Jacmel is no longer Jacmel," he had told the reporter. Comparing the place he'd re-created in his novels, the Jacmel of his youth, to the current Jacmel, which he had seen only on film and in photographs, he referred to the more contemporary Jacmel as a zombie.

For Depestre, a zombie has never been as simple a creation as the bleary-eyed villains of 1930s Hollywood B movies. Instead zombification is a state of deterioration based on the loss of one's *ti bonanj,* one's good angel, which turns one into a vacuous shell of one's former self. A case can be made that the Jacmel I am visiting now cannot help but be a slightly zombified version of its former self, having lost many of its own angels, among them one of its most adept literary chroniclers, to other shores.

Watching the carnival zombies on Sunday, I would also remember my uncle's wife, Tante Denise, waking me up one morning some twenty years ago to listen to the radio as an announcer reported that a few dozen zombies had been found wandering the northern hills of the country in a semicomatose state and that their loved ones should come claim them and take them home. As a child, it was those zombies that frightened me most, because they had been "discovered" not during the carnival season but during a less festive, more ordinary time. And aside from feeding them salt, at close range, as the legend says, there was no other way to help them return to their former selves, no rhyme to sing from a safe distance to make them go away.

Like many people, Tante Denise had concluded that these found zombies were actually former political prisoners—the likes of which had once been locked up by Charles Oscar Etienne—who were so mentally damaged by dictatorship-sponsored torture that they had become either crazy or slow. Tante Denise, like many others, had doubted that any relatives would go and get them, for fear of being locked up themselves.

On Sunday I would see a less frightening kind of zombie, the carnival kind. Watching its breath rise and fall beneath a white sheet, I would reach out and touch it, unafraid, for aside from loud music and lively dancing and street theater, this is what the carnival is for, I am learning: to exorcise old ghosts and fears.

With my hand on the zombie's back, I would lean forward and whisper, "Zombie, I'm not afraid of you. I know you're a human being." And I would wish that some of the relatives of the zombies found in the northern hills had gone and claimed them and had invented their own rhymes, songs, stories, and salty potions to bring them back to life.

There is music, Carnival. . . . The surf pounds; the
flowers bloom. Governments change, but Jacmel
remains the same.

CAROLE CLEAVER,
The New Leader

How to Get Your Own
Carnival Mask in Jacmel

HERE WAS AN invasion going on, a full-blown military operation in progress when some friends and I headed out in the night to find a soldier who had become a kind of legend in Jacmel. It was October 1994, and I was on one of my first trips back to Haiti since I had left at age twelve. My friends were filming a documentary and had asked me to come along. The documentary was about the recent return of President Aristide, who had been unseated in a military coup d'état seven months after his first inauguration as the first democratically elected Haitian president in 1991. Before we came, we had heard about "The Cowboy," Sergeant First Class Sam Makanani, a member of the United States special forces who had arrived in Haiti shortly before Aristide returned to the presidency. During Aristide's three years abroad, Haiti was ruled by a de facto military government, which through its soldiers and militiamen, called *attachés,* had tortured and murdered over five thousand people.

A symbol of the powerful U.S. Army, which was supposed to crush the more feeble yet repressive Haitian forces, Sergeant Makanani was described in hyperbolic terms even in the American press. In the *Washington Post,* Tod Robberson wrote, "A big green helicopter thundered down from the sky, creating a great burst of wind that made the date palms shake violently. Out stepped The Cowboy in full combat gear. And Jacmel's bad guys trembled."

There was a popular song at the time by the Haitian musical group Phantoms that declared Haiti a "Cowboy Country." This song might have served as fitting background music for Makanani's arrival. However, Makanani, later also called "Macaroni" by Jacmel's children, would earn his own songs and one of the greatest honors Jacmel has to offer: his own carnival mask.

In October 1994, there were paintings in arts and crafts shops all over Jacmel depicting Makanani's myth. Makanani with his feet on the neck of Haitian militiamen. Makanani riding his Humvee through the streets of Jacmel. Makanani escorting a group of *attachés* off to jail. Makanani playing the guitar surrounded by local children. Judging from those representations, it appears that the *Washington Post* journalist had only slightly exaggerated when he had written that "Sgt. 1st class Sam Makanani seems . . . the biggest hero ever to grace the shores of Jacmel."

"Why Jacmel residents chose Makanani as their hero is

anyone's guess," Robberson wrote. "But the fact that the spike-haired Hawaiian-born sergeant descended from the sky, in the biggest bird anyone had ever seen here, appears to have increased his almost god-like stature in the eyes of Jacmel's children. Upon seeing him on a balcony last Sunday, they burst into song: 'Makanani doesn't mess around. Makanani is one good guy. Makanani got them good!'"

When Makanani arrived in Jacmel, the town, as Robberson reported, was perhaps in need of heroes. Even before sharing in the national torment of the de facto government and the resulting international economic embargo, its affluent commercial ports had been shut down for decades by François "Papa Doc" Duvalier, who was punishing local businesspeople for not supporting him in the 1957 elections. (To further spite the Jacmelians, Duvalier had made one of his more famous speeches, a plea for international aid called the "Cri de Jacmel," the Cry from Jacmel, at the city's closed port.)

Most recently, Jacmel had been rocked by tropical storms, which had severely damaged the roads and bridges connecting it to the capital. Thus Makanani and the other soldiers who came with him were seen by some not only as rescuers but also potential builders. Makanani's being singled out for heroic status, however, might have had something to do with the fact that he was a man of color, fitting in somewhere between the mostly white military power structure and the locals. He also went after one of the town's most notorious killers, a real-life *chaloska* named Hughes Seraphin. When Makanani stormed Seraphin's house and captured him, he jokingly asked his commanding officer if he could shoot Seraphin while the local people watched. The reply from the commanding officer was no. However, Makanani's gesture, following his special forces dictum of "unconventional warfare," left a strong impression on his audience: that he was a powerful man who wanted to use his power to defend their side.

With that kind of legend surrounding him, even as my friends and I headed out into the night we were sure that we had little chance of actually finding Makanani. We had already spent an entire afternoon looking for him with no luck. The other American soldiers we had encountered along the way did not seem to want us to find him either. Some told us that he had left that very morning for the capital. Others told us that he was somewhere outside the city in the airport facility, which was off-limits to visitors. One muscle-bound older officer informed us that Makanani didn't exist, that he was a figment of the Haitians' imagination. The older man's companion told us that he didn't know him, nor did he want to. "We don't do things like that. We follow orders."

One of the local children, a huge Makanani fan, who was listening nearby had told us that Makanani sometimes cruised through town at night in his Humvee and that we were likely to run into him on patrol. And so we went out, circling the square, walking up and down stretches of the Baranquilla like devotees on a pilgrimage, hoping for a sighting.

It soon occurred to us that maybe Makanani had gone underground, keeping a low profile. Military life demands conformity. The nail that sticks out gets the hammer. In the capital, Captain Lawrence Rockwood, a counter-intelligence officer from the Tenth Mountain Division who had left his assigned barracks in the middle of the night to inspect a Haitian prison for human-rights abuses, would later be court-martialed. "Military justice is to justice what military music is to music," the statesman Georges Clemenceau had said. Maybe Makanani was playing a softer tune. When asked about his own legend, Makanani had told visiting journalists, "It's all lies." But perhaps military protocol had demanded that kind of answer.

I never did get to see Sergeant Makanani on that trip. Five years later, however, a few days before the national carnival, I would see a picture of the Makanani mask, which had premiered in the Jacmel carnival the year after he had arrived. It was a giant papier-mâché construction, a cross between a werewolf and a tiger, a near replica of a pre-Hispanic pottery mask with ears sticking out like TV antennas in opposite directions. The mask, as well as the costume that accompanied it, was covered in the Stars and Stripes. A long paper tongue hung out from between the sharp teeth of the growling beast. On the tongue were written the words *"Makanani pran yo."* Makanani got them.

I don't know if Makanani ever saw his mask stroll down the Baranquilla in the carnival parade before the

U.S. forces were pulled out of Haiti. But when the first Makanani mask was made part of the carnival, says Divers, "For better or worse, Makanani became included not only in the history, but also the legend of Jacmel. When the mask goes by in the parade and visitors ask, 'Who is that?,' people will have to tell his story."

Oh Jacmel! You breathe like a human being

. . . to inspire the fiercest passions.

ROMUALTH NELSON

Refuge in Jacmel

W HEN TWO TOURISTS and their driver were murdered in Jacmel in January 2000, thousands of people took to the streets to protest the killings.

Fernand and Evelyne Mellier and their daughter Celine had come to Jacmel from Le Cateau, France, hoping to buy land to build a house near the beach. The Melliers had been sleeping in their rooms at Cyvadier Plage Hotel when a group of men came to tell them at 4:00 A.M. that their driver, Aspril Aubin, had suddenly taken ill and had sent for them. Fernand Mellier went with the men, leaving his wife and teenage daughter at the hotel. Three hours later, the men returned, announcing to the women that Mellier wanted them to come to him. The mother refused to go, staying behind as her daughter went to join the father. Later that day, the bodies of Fernand and Celine Mellier and Aspril Aubin were found at different locations outside Jacmel.

This crime shocked Jacmelians, who are so confident in the safety of their town that they have signs painted on the walls declaring that Jacmel has 100 percent security. Not that there is a larger police presence in Jacmel than anywhere else in Haiti; Jacmel is just calmer, cleaner, less populated. These types of things just don't happen here.

Among the Jacmelians who took to the streets to protest were religious leaders, health professionals, businesspeople, schoolchildren and their teachers. They carried signs that said FIND THE CRIMINALS SO THESE CRIMES WILL NEVER BE REPEATED and VIOLENCE, NO! Businesses were closed during the march, and among the organizers were the Office of Tourism and city hall officials. The killing of Fernand and Celine Millier and Aspril Aubin threatened to destroy Jacmel's stature as a peaceful haven, not only for foreigners but for Haitians—some of whom often come to Jacmel for the weekend and others who, tired of living in the capital and abroad, have permanently relocated here.

A Frenchman I meet at the Alliance Française (the French Institute) of Jacmel a few nights before carnival is still thinking about the murder, a year later; however, it has not deterred him from coming.

Skinny, pensive, and middle-aged, Bertrand Goussé has been a freelance photographer for thirty years. He has traveled all over the Caribbean and is working on a book of photographs of Haiti. He has been in the country for two months, and in Jacmel for six days. The night Rodney and I run into him, at an outdoor exposition of carnival masks in the courtyard of the Alliance Française, he has just written a letter to his daughter in Paris about his visit to Haiti.

"Darling," he wrote, "I know you are worried about me because of all that you've heard. I know the impression is really bad. All I can tell you is that the more I see of Haiti the more I realize that this is in many ways a country like any other, a country one must discover."

The night that Goussé is there, the Alliance Française is full of local people getting a preview of Sunday's carnival. The courtyard's stone walls are covered with masks, and the yard itself crowded with costumes hanging on poles of different sizes, each looking like a scarecrow in the middle of a field.

As I make my way into the courtyard, leaving Rodney up front chatting with an old friend of his from Port-au-Prince, the first thing that catches my attention is the Yawe, a giant mass of cowhide half covered with red satin. On Sunday, as the Yawe strolls down the street in the carnival parade—this time with a person inside—people will come forward, blow loud whistles, and pound on it with sticks. The whole scene, with the revelers blowing whistles and pounding, and the Yawe sometimes cowering and sometimes attempting to run away, will seem like a blend between a rodeo and a bullfight in which the bull has already been caught but has not quite surrendered.

According to the journalist Louis Pélissier Baptiste, the thrashing of the Yawe is a re-creation of a hunting scene, a shared memory of the Arawak Indians, the African slaves, and the French buccaneers, in which a wild bull that has already been shot with arrows and wounded is still attempting to run away. How this interactive costume came to be called a Yawe no one is quite sure. Divers thinks it might have something to do with Jacmel's eighteenth-century Jewish settlers—businessmen from the Dutch islands—who may have come up with the display as a reenactment of the sacrifice of a bull to Yahweh, or God.

The Yawe has its parallel in the Lu Bov Fint, or the false ox of Italian carnivals. Made of wood and iron and draped with red cloth, the Lu Bov Fint costume was worn by one or two people, like a modern-day mascot suit, and then chased through town by revelers. In the Italian carnival, the hunt of the Lu Bov Fint is meant to represent an old custom in which an ox was slaughtered on the day before Lent to give the poor a rare chance to eat meat.

Next to the Yawe is a ghost, a skeletal mask painted in white over black cloth. In the carnival on Sunday, the ghosts will stand in the middle of crossroads and point in the direction of the cemetery.

A group of schoolgirls are standing in front of the ghost giggling while reaching up as if to touch the ghost's face. One of the girls tries to pry forward a younger relative who is clinging to her legs with one hand and covering her face with the other.

Between the ghost and the Yawe, I spot Paula Hyppolite, a jewelry maker who lives in the mountains of Cap

Rouge. Born in Port-au-Prince, Hyppolite had moved to the United States when she was sixteen. When she became pregnant with her first child, at twenty-one, she returned to Haiti to give birth because she wanted her child to feel connected to her country. She then left the child with family members and went back to New York to make enough money to support both the child and herself. There she worked as a cabdriver in the Bedford Stuyvesant section of Brooklyn, one of the few women on the job. When the child rejoined her, she became a single mother who for seven years dreamed of returning to her homeland.

"My body was in New York," she says, "but my soul was here. I had to come back to connect the two."

As we sit in a corner of the courtyard talking, we both occasionally look up to examine a mask or costume. I can't keep my eyes off a large gorilla head with a red crown because it reminds me of a Jean-Michel Basquiat painting. Paula is staring at "The Tongue of Jacmel," a long piece of cowhide reaching from the top of a pole down to the floor. The "Tongue" is meant as a commentary on the people of Jacmel, who as legend has it are great talkers.

When she finally returned to Haiti in 1996, intending to stay for good, Paula Hyppolite took a bus from the capital, up the "Friendship Road," which winds around the mountains leading to Jacmel. Looking outside the bus window at the treeless mountains, she began to cry.

"All my fears were confirmed," she says. "The mountains were bare."

When a woman on the bus reached over to tap her on the shoulder and ask her what was wrong, she somehow managed to whisper, sobbing, "The mountains are so bare."

The woman thought she was crazy.

Paula leased a piece of land in Cap Rouge, where she settled. Shocked by the high price of fruits and vegetables, she grew her own. Among other things, she grows broccoli, which few others have ever tried in Cap Rouge.

"It's still a wonder for me to put a seed in the ground and get a plant or a tree," she says. She travels all over Haiti looking for pods and seeds and tree branches, which she uses to make her necklaces and bracelets, as a tribute to the lost trees. She will be selling her jewelry in town during the carnival weekend.

Paula's eyes wander up again, this time to a cluster of three papier-mâché mules draped with yellow satin cloth bordered with lace. As in medieval feasts of the ass, during carnival the mules paradoxically become symbols of luxury, almost like exotic pets. The rest of the year, they are simply pack animals, carrying heavy loads up and down mountains, across rivers and plains, while being pulled and tugged in every direction. The unenviable condition of the mule led the novelist Zora Neale Hurston to align them with women, whom she pegged as the Caribbean's other beasts of burden. There is a scene in C. L. R. James's *The Black Jacobins* in which a colonist asks a slave beating his mule, "Why do you ill treat your mule that way?" And the slave replies that he does so because "when I do not work I am beaten." The mule was *his* slave.

At carnival, at least temporarily, the wrongs committed against the mule are symbolically redressed.

PAULA HAS TO go see about her jewelry, which is on display at another exposition house down the street. I continue my stroll through the courtyard, stopping in front of a maypole over fifteen feet tall. The maypole is covered from top to bottom with satin ribbons, woven together in various intricate symmetrical designs.

During the trip sponsored by the Ministry of Haitians Living Abroad, Michaelle Craan, the carnival narrator and ringmistress, a carnival organizing committee member, and a passionate promoter of Jacmel, had arranged for our group to see a *trese riban,* a maypole dance, at Jacmel's city hall. Working in male-female pairs, the maypole dancers each held the end of a ribbon, the other end of which was attached to the top of the pole, then rhythmically crossed each other, ducking under and skipping over the ribbons, while braiding them into a gorgeous mosaic around the pole.

The wooden beam that formed the centerpiece for the dance had reminded me of the *mai sauvage,* a type of post erected in French villages as a symbol of freedom during that country's revolution. Perhaps this is how the maypole made its way to Jacmel, or as part of medieval-derived agricultural May Day celebrations, which the colonists probably maintained on the island. Like the informal *maryaj pou dis* of Haiti's carnival, mock marriages were performed during May Day celebrations, marriages that were supposed to last a year and a day.

During carnival, according to Divers, men dressed as women would sometimes perform the maypole dance, taking on the role of May queens celebrating a good harvest, or greeting the arrival of springtime. This might explain the pair of satin gowns hanging next to the maypole in the middle of the Alliance Française courtyard.

Inside the Alliance Française building itself are paintings and crafts for sale, purses made out of calabashes, serving trays covered with giant parrots and hibiscus blossoms, and frames shaped like the doors and windows of Jacmel's gingerbread houses. A young man from the art institute in Port-au-Prince is arguing loudly with one of the painters in the exhibition, who has caught him explaining his paintings to someone else.

"Only I can explain this painting," the artist says.

"When you put something out in the world, everyone has the right to interpret it," the student says.

The artist will not give in.

"I made it. I know exactly what it is and what each thing stands for."

"Yours is only one interpretation," the student insists.

Goussé is leaving, disappearing into the night with his letter to his daughter in his pocket. In a corner near the door is a small painting done in soft-hued beige and black, as if to duplicate a sepia-toned photograph. The painting shows a beach, a few palm trees, and three people with their backs to the canvas viewer, their faces turned to the beach.

The artist is standing next to his painting, as if guarding it with his life.

"What is it called?" I ask.

"Refuge in Jacmel," he replies.

I return to the courtyard, drawn by a mask of Lucifer, the scowling red face crowned with two long horns that make him look almost like a bull. In the book *Masks: Faces of Culture,* which accompanied a mask exhibition at the Saint Louis Art Museum, the authors, John W. Nunley and Cara McCarty, saw the Jacmel devil mask as a representation of the Yoruba war deity, Ogun, who is also the god of metal and iron.

Also watching the devil is Papayo, who has an arts and crafts shop near city hall. The shop is a regular hangout for neighborhood men who do not go to the restaurants and cafés in town. Some of the men are artists who make the miniature houses, beaded curtains, and paintings that Papayo sells. Others are just unemployed and chat with Papayo through the walls of the shop between visitors. When the nuns from the nearby Catholic school send lunch to Papayo for keeping an eye on the school at night, he shares it with all the men, sometimes having none left for himself.

I met Papayo one morning while he was sweeping the street in front of his shop, mumbling to himself. We got into a conversation about Jacmel and the fact that it seems to inspire and draw so many artists.

"Jacmel produces lots of artists because it's small and all our umbilical cords are tied together," he said.

Papayo had returned to Haiti at forty-one after working as a fisherman in Bogotá, Colombia, for many years. He considers himself a bridge between the public and the artists and craftspeople who need time and money to work. If you ask him for anything that is not in his shop, he tells you quickly, "I'll talk to the guys about it."

Recently he has been collecting loose roots from old trees, some of them washing up on the beach, others just lying in the middle of mountain roads after a heavy rain. He has been letting the roots stand in his shop, taking their own shape as they dry. One large root looks like an octopus. Another looks like a crowd of people. The roots are like Rorschach inkblot tests, each person seeing something different in them. Papayo is the first vendor I have seen with so many of the untreated roots, a relatively new form of natural found-object sculpture here.

Papayo is staring at the Lucifer mask in the Alliance Française Institute courtyard with great fascination.

After a while I ask him, "What do you see?"

As if quoting Marlow from Conrad's *Heart of Darkness*, he replies, "I see the devil of hunger, the devil of misery, the devil of sadness, the devil of greed."

TOWARD THE END of the evening, Ronald Mews stops by. Known for his modern—some might say postmodern— canvases and his own singular kind of found-object art, Mews moved to Jacmel after years of living in New York, Canada, and Port-au-Prince. Earlier that day, I had run into him on the road near Cyvadier Beach, on his way to buy a coffin for one of his neighbors, a young girl who had died after a sudden illness. An easygoing man with a concentrated glare, a comfortable laugh, and a passion for social and political commentary, Mews is often seen around town in shorts and a T-shirt with a fanny pack attached to his waist, his long salt-and-pepper beard making him instantly recognizable. His work has been part of group and single expositions in Haiti, the United States, Canada, France, and Mexico. The first time I had met him, six months ago, a friend had taken me to his home, between a brook and a small burial ground outside of Jacmel, and even before showing me his studio he had brought me to see the old tombstones behind his house. During my stays in Jacmel I would often spot him around town hauling rocks and cement for a local school or the studio he was completing on the hill above his house. Early in the morning, he could be seen chauffeuring his two sons and a group of local children to school in an open-backed truck, and in the afternoon, stopping briefly to chat with acquaintances and younger painters, who all call him Atis la (The Artist), as he drove through town on his way to pick up the children.

Rodney and I ask Mews if we can see his studio. We agree on the next evening. A large barn-style room with a high tin roof, the studio is crowded with half-finished and completed paintings, as well as pieces of furniture that he has recently built. Striking in its range of themes, colors, and materials, Mews's work is hard to categorize. Some Haitian critics call it abstract because he often uses ambiguous forms; however, his figures are often recognizable, such as the open wings of a devil in one painting, or the pale, fragile-looking crosses and hearts in others. Mews characterizes his work as a kind of improvisation, like jazz, but also as an attempt to re-create a common memory, a way to fill in historical gaps.

"Haitian history teaches you political history," he says, his voice competing with the wailing cicadas and grasshoppers outside his studio. "For example, what did a Haitian do before independence? What did he wear? What did he eat? How did he bathe? If you ask me, I am not able to tell you. That makes me feel amputated, so I allow myself to fill in the space, to create images that are missing."

In the studio, I stroll from one set of works in progress to the next, from a series of small paintings made to fit trefoiled frames to a collage of flattened metal attached to an old burlap sack.

Mews started painting as a child, using brushes discarded by his father. When he was thirteen, he quit school to have a closer look at his environment, to climb trees and bathe in streams, to use a magnifying glass to observe what he calls microlandscapes, ants darting in and out of small holes in the ground, tiny plants and flowers, dust balls. As an adult, he made those miniature vistas the subject of his work. But even though his paintings were reproduced directly from his observations of Haitian soil, his work was rejected by some Haitians because it did not fit the popular "naïf" style of other self-taught Haitian artists.

He moved to New York, for years working as a bartender in jazz clubs, befriending musicians, artists, and writers, among them *Silence of the Lambs* author Thomas Harris. During the day, he read art books and visited galleries and museums, finding himself surrounded by American pop art, which he considered liberating, he says, because "I saw people who were using many different ways to express themselves as artists."

In the studio, I spot a collection of doors—French, louvered, and shuttered doors that he has rescued from old rural and urban Jacmel houses before they were demolished. He has collected the doors, he says, as a way to preserve the old architecture of Jacmel, but also because doors represent openings, passages, and the *Vodou* spirit Legba, who is the guardian of the crossroads.

"Haitians have always been on the avant-garde of many things," he says, running his fingers through the slanted louvers of one pale green door. "For example, Haitian craftspeople have used tin cans to make lamps, motor-oil containers to make sculptures. Before Europeans were using collage as artistic expression, poor Haitians were using newspapers and magazines to decorate the walls of their houses. They used *Paris Match,* the *New York Times,* and *Le Nouvelliste,* so that you would have a Haitian peasant lying in bed with his toes in Brigitte Bardot's eyes."

As Mews's laughter echoes throughout the room, a rooster crows from somewhere. I call these twenty-four-hour roosters, the ones that don't wait until dawn to crow.

"In Haiti we take surrealism for granted," Mews continues, still laughing. "That's why French surrealists like André Breton came to Haiti to see what was going on here. Why do you have all those painters who paint large fruits, forests, jungles, when the trees have all but disappeared?"

"Why?" I ask, as if awaiting the answer to a riddle.

Mews replies, "Because we paint what is missing in our lives. We paint to fill the gap. Since there is a lack of food, we paint giant fruits. Since there are few trees, we paint jungles."

Behind Mews is a set of drums, which he has been making with the help of local drum makers. Creating drums as art is not all that common. Mews is doing this to right a wrong, he says, to heal a painful memory. In the 1940s, the Catholic Church, with help from the Haitian government, organized a nationwide "antisuperstition" campaign in which drums used in *Vodou* ceremonies were burned, and mapou trees, which are not only among the largest and shadiest trees in Haiti but are also considered sacred, were cut down.

"Why Jacmel?" Rodney asks Mews. Why did he, a well-known artist who could live anywhere in the world, come to live in the woods in Jacmel?

He came to Jacmel, he said, to be near some basic natural elements of life—streams, waters, mountains, a cemetery—and to better know the "outside people" of Haiti.

As I listened to him, I thought of something that the Yugoslavian-born poet Charles Simic had once said, that an artist should know what it is like to live among those "walking in broad daylight, as well as among those hiding behind closed shutters."

A few days later, Mews's wife, Consuela, would show me a picture of him taken during carnival the year before. A group of local people had stopped by his house on their way to the carnival parade. His mother-in-law had brought makeup and costumes to help the group stand out. In the picture, Mews is meticulously applying lipstick to an older woman's face as though it were one of his favorite canvases.

A green lizard darts behind Mews now, jumping onto one of his unfinished paintings. For a moment, it seems as if the lizard has always been there, as if it belongs there.

Mews himself will not go to the carnival, but he hosts a few dozen friends and family members from the capital who come to attend.

"I don't need to go to carnival," he says. "An artist's, a writer's imagination is already a carnival."

You're not yet satisfied with the carnival
But Ash Wednesday will soon be here.

MANNO CHARLEMAGNE,
Lamayòt

Carnival of the Trees

W HEN I WAS a child living in Port-au-Prince,
along with the *chaloska* there was another carnival character that came to find me, even though I never
went looking for it. It was the *lamayòt*. The *lamayòt* is a
secret, a benign Pandora's box one willingly unveils for
one's pleasure.

Every Sunday afternoon during the carnival season,
there would be a visit from someone whom I guess you
would call a *lamayòteur*, usually a man walking from house
to house with a box or a sack in which there was something children would pay a penny to have a look at. Even
though I was not allowed to go see the *lamayòt*, I would
watch the neighborhood children take turns peeking
inside the sack or box and then listen to them describe
what they had seen. Often the *lamayòt* was an interesting
object—a large marble, a prism—but sometimes it was a
small animal—a lizard, a frog, a turtle, or a snake, a marvel for city kids.

Later I would notice that the word *lamayòt* was also used in a broader context in adult conversations. If someone tried to show you something too quickly, it was a *lamayòt*. If you were buying something sight unseen, you were getting a *lamayòt*. A too short rendezvous with one's lover was a *lamayòt,* as was a false personal or political promise.

Anyone who has ever been to Haiti can see the country's deforestation. So much so that one might feel that in Haiti, trees are *lamayòt*.

The first time I returned to Haiti as an adult, in the 1990s, I was shocked that there were any trees left at all. Having read so much about the countless number of trees cut down and never replanted each year, I was expecting a desert. Part of the reason I am so drawn to Jacmel is that compared to the rest of Haiti, it is relatively green. Palms and coconut trees line the coast; banana, almond, and mandarin groves block some roadside houses from view, and in the mountains above Jacmel, in an area called Seguin, there is a pine forest, and its trees are among the most remarkable in Haiti.

I had read two articles about the pine forest, officially called Parc de la Visite, written by two different Americans, Tequila Minsky and J. P. Slavin, who had separately walked there from the hills above Port-au-Prince. Last summer my friend Fedo, who was then traveling with me, and I were both intrigued with the idea of seeing the pine forest and decided to go.

Short on time, we drove a borrowed pickup through a series of steep mountains and craggy trails. ("People always write about bad roads in Haiti," a friend of mine once said. "The roads are bad so you can truly appreciate the beauty of where you're going once you get there. These roads are there so one can *earn* the beauty.")

As we climb higher and higher up the side of one particular mountain, I feel we are really earning the beauty with each lurch and pull of the car. Around us is a tableau of other mountain ranges where beans, yams, and coffee are planted and harvested on precipitous slopes. Small villages and graveyards dangle precariously on the edge of high cliffs, between ravine and sky. We struggle past one isolated house after another, greeting elders and children, who sometimes stroll alongside the slow-moving car or hop in the back on their way somewhere else. They advise us about spots on the path to avoid, while playfully questioning us.

Are we heading to the Parc de la Visite?

Yes.

Are we reporters? Public officials?

We proudly say we are Haitians trying to see more of the country.

My friend Fedo, who owns a translation company in Miami, had lived in Haiti until he was sixteen and then had moved to Canada, then the United States. He enjoys the conversations so much that by the time we part with our passengers, we feel as though we have known them all our lives. When they leave us, they tell us to *ankouraje,* take heart, as we are not too far from our destination. Seguin is just around the corner, distance being a matter of perception, attitude, and determination. Time too becomes subjective. Has it really been an hour, and have we covered only one mile? We stop often so I can photograph graveyards, which Fedo thinks is a morbid preoccupation. He prefers to photograph the broader landscapes, the ocean we are leaving behind, the mountains lined up in uneven rows. I think these mountains, as spectacular as they are, make for boring pictures since you can never get their full breadth, which appears flat on paper.

We dread crossroads, those forks on the path with no signs. One wrong turn can lead us back to whence we came or, even worse, all the way to Port-au-Prince. At one of the crossroads, we pick up Marlène, a nineteen-year-old who is on her way to visit her family in a small village near Seguin. Marlène is chic in her blue jeans, striped blouse, and dark wraparound glasses. She moved down from the mountains to study dressmaking in Jacmel. Even though her craft, once essential to Haitian life, is slowly being rendered obsolete by the flood of used ready-made clothes from abroad, she is certain that she will earn a living by making clothes for people who still crave a tailor-made dress and are able to pay for it.

It turns out that Marlène is the most popular woman in Jacmel. She rolls down the window to chat with everyone; they all not only know her by name but know her father and stepmother and three brothers as well. When she arrives at her house, she stops to introduce us to her father and then, fearing that we might get lost, continues with us the rest of the way.

The road levels off by the time we reach Seguin. From the steps of a white-and-turquoise building that seems like the town hall, a mason lodge, a community center, and a church all at once, we can already see the outline of the pine forest. The turquoise-and-white building is capped with an upward-aimed arrow on top of the steeple, where there usually would have been a cross. An arrow is a "sign of war, token of aggression and manful self-assertion," according to art historian Robert Farris Thompson, but perhaps, at over five thousand feet, it is also a poignant reminder that in this part of the country, at least, heaven is the next highest place.

A woman is screaming in the distance, running toward a new gravel road in mid-construction. A presidential project, the road will connect Seguin to the hills above Port-au-Prince. Soon the trail that the two Americans, Tequila Minsky and J. P. Slavin, had walked will be a paved thoroughfare, bringing along with it public transportation and a shorter journey to the market for many vendors who have to travel on foot with heavy baskets on their heads.

Marlène asks someone about the screaming woman.

"There was an accident," a child says. One of the first camions to attempt the road had turned over and fallen into a ravine. A few people had been injured. Fearing the victims' families' wrath, the driver had fled. Now this woman who was screaming as though the ache of the accident was going through her own body was heading down the road to see about her loved one.

As we approach the pine forest, we pass gardens of giant rocks jutting out of the ground. The rocks form fields of natural sculptures, some split down the middle to look like mouths screaming up at the sky. In her essay for the Web site Windows on Haiti, Tequila Minsky says that these rocks left her "gasping in wonderment. The locals call them *kraze dan* (breaking teeth)"—perhaps because they look like teeth, but also because one would surely break one's teeth were one to land on one of them. Looking at these stones, I can't help but think that these rocks are convincing evidence that the earth is a living entity, the oceans and rivers her blood, the soil her skin, and the stones, her bones.

The temperature has dropped considerably. It now feels like a late fall day to our bare arms and legs. Some of the people who pass us on the way home from their fields are wearing full-length wool winter coats. Marlène leaves us to return home. She will stop on the way to visit a friend. We make an appointment to meet up with her on our way down the next afternoon.

On the edge of the park is Auberge de la Visite, a small ranch with two houses with stone walls and a red tin roof. A German shepherd greets us as we drive through the gate. Aside from the dog, the place seems deserted. As we go in farther, a man appears. It is Gerald, the manager. Lucky for us, since we had no reservation, there are no other guests here.

The night comes quickly, everything beyond the front porch of the inn blending into darkness. If not for a kerosene lamp, we wouldn't even see our own hands. Just as suddenly, it begins to rain, a loud thundering rain that reminds me of hailstorms pounding the tin roofs of my childhood, each drop landing with a clamoring thump, like a million hands clapping.

Inside we play dominoes with Gerald and Nadège, who works as a cook at the inn, and listen to the rain. We try to coax them into telling us odd tales about past visitors with no success.

I read the guest book.

"It is with sadness that I will go down the mountain, but with a desire to return," wrote a Nick Bishop. Someone else has written in French, "I left a bit of my soul in these impenetrable mountains."

I fall asleep to the sound of the rain, soothing in its insistence after a while, no lightning or thunder, just rain.

By 5:00 a.m., roosters are crowing—these are not twenty-four-hour roosters—and the sun is so bright that it looks as though it has already been up for hours. Yet it is cold, like an early-winter morning. I follow the example of the peasant women I see walking on the nearby trail and wrap one of my aunt Ilyana's scarves, a gift from our last visit together, around my head to keep it warm. After breakfast, we stroll downhill past a chicken coop, through

a beanfield. Fedo stops to photograph the white flowers between the bean leaves. Having grown up in the southern city of Les Cayes and in Port-au-Prince, he is more or less a city boy. That legume vines can blossom into flowers astounds him.

We start down on the open road, flattened and covered with gravel, not yet paved. The accident must have happened farther down on a less even plane. We take a side path into the forest. There are wild cacti among the pines, ferns, and shrubs, surrounded by a cushion of pine needles and cones still damp from last night's rain. The aroma of pines envelops us and a small flock of birds peek down on us from the top of the trees as though we are *lamayòts*.

At first we walk in circles, taking trails that lead us again and again to the same spot. I review my reading about pines. There are about two hundred pine species in the world. Though they grow relatively quickly, some pines can last as long as four thousand years. Pines produce both female and male cones, the female cones being larger and more obvious than the males. The male cones bear pollen, which fertilizes the female cones to form seeds. The young seeds may travel hundreds of feet in the wind, away from the parent trees. Like immigrants from their birthplace.

In the park are both hard and soft pines, of various sizes and shapes. Some are over a hundred feet tall and others much shorter, with thinner trunks.

We hear the sound of water crashing against rock and

head toward it. Around a series of layered cascades are caves and grottoes. Before independence, slaves would meet in forests like this one to plan attacks against their masters. During the nineteen-year American occupation of Haiti (from 1915 to 1934), people who wanted to avoid forced labor would meet in forests and in the dry galleries of grottoes and caves to organize sovereignty brigades. The expatriates who invaded Haiti in the 1960s, those who wanted to unseat the dictator François Duvalier, relied on the cover of densely packed trees and forests to shield them from view. So much so that Duvalier burned down an entire forest in the north in order to establish a cordon sanitaire, so future revolutionaries would have no place to hide. The fact that it was Duvalier's son Jean-Claude who decreed this pine forest protected territory in 1983 seems ironic at best, a small act of redemption, perhaps, for his father's elimination of so many other trees.

A man from the park office is sawing away at a fallen pine on the forest grounds. Since it is illegal to cut them down, the only pines that leave this place now are the ones that are ancient enough to have dropped by themselves. Pines make the best lumber, it is said, and their pulpwood makes paper.

In his November 1999 article in *Food & Home* magazine, the journalist J. P. Slavin reports that the Haitian scholar and *Vodou* priest Max Beauvoir wrote to him about the park in Seguin, saying, "All of these mountains are referred to as *'boutilyes,'* which is the land of the first ancestors. It is not unusual to see people who go there to come down from their horses, remove their shoes, and kneel down to pray to their fore-fathers."

The Haitian novelist Jacques Stephen Alexis, who was ambushed by Duvalier loyalists during an expedition to overthrow Duvalier père's regime, wrote before he died, "The trees fall from time to time but the voice of the forest never loses its power." And he was—is—right. The trilling of a midday breeze blowing through the pines suggests human voices. Even the echo of my voice, bounced against the trees, sounds like a series of other voices all together.

As the forest thins out, we find ourselves on the ridge of a massive canyon. Clouds hover above and below us, the cirrus like giant brushstrokes overhead and the cumulus crawling in circular puffs underneath. We are playing the ultimate game of *lamayòt,* the clouds at times blocking portions of the valley, at other times giving us a full view of the rivers and hills and waterfalls below. Devil's confusion, as Toni Morrison might say; for a minute all I see is a lush carpet of green over everything.

WE MAKE IT back to the auberge in the early afternoon and begin our trip back down the mountain. On the way we pick up Marlène in front of her father's house. She fills us in on the camion accident. It was worse than we had first heard. Several people had died, including the son of the woman we'd heard screaming. As we travel down the mountains, Marlène stops to say good-bye to everyone she meets.

"A mountain road is like life," she says. "You never know where you'll end up."

It is significant that a country as sorrowful as ours should have so many and such joyous fiestas. Their . . . brilliance and excitement, the enthusiasm with which we take part, all suggest that without them we would explode.

OCTAVIO PAZ

Carnival Friday

O^{N THE WEEKEND} of carnival, Haiti is experiencing a national crisis. A few weeks before, former president Jean-Bertrand Aristide had been reelected, and in protest the opposition had formed its own parallel government, an act that some predicted could lead to civil war. During the national carnival weekend, as on so many others that preceded it, the country's concerns remain the same, with worries over inflation, unemployment, illiteracy, political corruption, soil erosion, and contraband trade. In other words, the country is wrestling with the quartet of devils that Papayo thought he saw in the yard of the Alliance Française a few days earlier: the devil of hunger, the devil of misery, the devil of sadness, the devil of greed. One would be hard-pressed, however, to find evidence of any of this in Jacmel on Friday night, where the opening of the national carnival festivities is marked by a large fireworks display, which will be repeated every night throughout the weekend. Each time the fireworks go off, they remind me of a bumper sticker I once spotted on a Haitian-owned car in Miami. NO ROADS, NO ELECTRICITY, NO RUNNING WATER, NO TELEPHONES, read the bumper sticker, BUT I STILL LOVE HAITI.

Earlier in the day, I had been to one of Jacmel's definite marvels, a trio of turquoise pools beneath a giant waterfall in a place called Bassin Bleu. Aladin, the man who owned the rope that was needed to descend along the slippery wet rocks into the blue-green pools, had said something that was the equivalent of that bumper sticker: "A love for a place like Haiti is a love that cannot be explained. It has its good and bad side, but at times the bad part can make you love the good part even more. You love her. You hate her. You pity her. You want to protect her. That's how it is with Haiti."

I MEET UP with Michelet Divers again at the Hotel de la Place the Friday afternoon before the carnival. The terrace is crowded now, with new Haitian and foreign faces. More visitors are walking to and from the bar, and up and down the staircase leading to the rooms upstairs. Across the street, in the square, a boom box is playing a medley of old and new carnival songs. Students on vacation until the following Tuesday are playing cards or strolling together along the Allée des Amoureux, the Alley of Lovers. Older people lean on canes as they sit on the square's benches, watching the visitors from the capital and elsewhere who wander aimlessly past them, their heads twisting here and there as if to take it all in at once—the music, the trees, the mountains, always visible in the distance. In the gazebo in the middle of the square, two men have set up a pinball machine that one can play for a price, and along with some of the vendors of candy, chewing gum, and cigarettes are cooks setting up to make the powdered-sugar-covered banana fritters that one can only find for sale on street corners during carnival.

At an intersection diagonally across from the Hotel de la Place, a group of young people have set up a table of games, the most popular being the one with the water jar and the bottle cap. In the center at the bottom of a large water-filled jar is a bottle cap. The goal of the game is to drop a coin through the water so that it lands inside the bottle cap. If you win, you earn all the money at the bottom of the jar, or some other prize, like a key chain or a stuffed animal. If you lose, your money remains at the bottom of the jar.

I remember this game from childhood. My cousins and I would re-create it at home, taking turns at dropping the same penny into a jar of water and taking the penny out with a spoon, only to drop it in again. It was always a thrill for me to watch the coin float from the top of the jar to the bottom, sometimes coming close and touching the bottle cap, sometimes landing inside. When I was younger, I thought it was a matter of chance, getting the penny in the bottle cap, but now I am convinced that it is a matter of manipulated physics, hard water versus soft, plain water versus salted water, which forces the coin to float anywhere but straight down.

I think of the Russian critic Mikhail Bakhtin, who wrote that games are closely related to the future, to destiny. Carnival games, he wrote, are a "condensed formula of life and of the historic process: fortune and misfortune, gain and loss, crowning and uncrowning."

We are sharing common experiences with the water jar and bottle cap game, Divers and I, when I notice that he is somewhat preoccupied. His mind is elsewhere. He appears nervous.

"It is the carnival," he says. He has concerns. A few disputes have developed between some of the carnival groups and city hall. The bands involved in the disputes are threatening to sit out this carnival. Divers has been up since the night before, negotiating with the bands, and is still waiting to hear whether or not some bands will be participating on Sunday.

"I do not want the carnival to go off badly," he says, taking a few peanuts from a small bag that I had purchased at the bar inside. "Because if the carnival goes off badly, it looks bad for Jacmel. Jacmel's reputation is at stake here. We are going to be on display. Whenever the carnival does not go well, even if our visitors from elsewhere are satisfied, the Jacmelians are embarrassed, because we know we can do better."

"What would be the ideal carnival?" I ask him.

"I don't know what the perfect carnival is," he says,

"but I know when it's not good. I suppose a very good carnival would have a lot of color, a lot of music. Lots of people enjoying themselves and no one getting hurt."

"Do you think you'll have a very good carnival on Sunday?" I ask.

"The committee is working hard to see that it happens," he says. "I am anxious because I like to have everything go smoothly. I do not want anything to go badly on Sunday. We had a very big disaster once."

The disaster Divers is talking about happened a few years ago: a fire in the middle of the carnival parade.

"Sunday parade was terminated abruptly," Carole Cleaver, a longtime resident of Jacmel, wrote in an article for the *New Leader* magazine, "when the float bearing the carnival queen caught fire. Members of the Jouvenceaux, the local band that accompanied her highness, leaped from the pyre, abandoning their instruments. The crowd saved the queen, carried away adjacent parked cars whose gas tanks might have caused an explosion, then stood back to watch the flames. By the time one fire engine arrived, the fire had burned itself out."

In his book, Divers describes the fire as a rare unfortunate incident that thankfully has never been repeated. According to Divers, the other carnivals of the military de facto years, particularly the one that took place in the spring of 1994, were perhaps just as disastrous as the one in the year of the fire. However, the people made the most of them, because they were necessary distractions to their daily struggles.

The year 1994, he writes, "was the worst political crisis in the history of this turbulent little country. A carnival during an international economic embargo. High inflation. High hopes. Industries in trouble. Worrisome misery. A town without electricity. A youth without guidance. And the people must enjoy themselves, must dance."

That spring, says Divers, the musical groups had even larger speakers, blaring their carnival anthems even more defiantly. The voices sang louder, the people danced longer, as if to rebel against the extremely difficult circumstances.

So is the Jacmel carnival a contemporary bread-and-circus prescription for keeping the masses happy, as Carole Cleaver had stated in her article?

"Carnival has always been a break from life," says Divers. "This is a country where people are poor in money perhaps, but rich in culture. Carnival is our chance to show our kind of wealth. If people were only concerned about bread, would you ever have any artistic expression at all? Would people paint, write, make music? It's like the proverb says, 'After the dance, the drum is heavy.' But during the dance, you're not thinking about the weight of the drum. You forget your troubles and have a good time."

THAT NIGHT, RODNEY and I attend the pageant that will crown city hall's carnival queen. The contest is being held at Samba Night Club, an open-air dance hall. Rows of tables and chairs are lined up in the courtyard, surrounding the ring-shaped stage, which is bordered by red and white balloons and a large banner for the radio station Vision 2000, the official sponsor. Fireworks fill the sky overhead, momentarily outshining a plethora of stars. An Elton John song blares from the loudspeakers over the stage.

"I believe in love," sings Elton. "It's all we've got."

Journalist Pierre Nazon Beaulière, the liaison between Vision 2000 and city hall, is at the bar. Twelve contestants signed up for the contest, he reports; however, he does not expect all twelve to show. "The shyness of young women, we are struggling against it," says Beaulière.

A few of the contestants arrive carrying bags filled with costume changes. They skip off to a room behind the bar after greeting Beaulière.

The main prize, of course, will be to become one of the queens of the carnival, the canonical title being Miss Carnaval Sud-Est, Miss Carnival Southeast. The queen gets to be feted at the official stand on Sunday next to foreign diplomats and local public officials. She will also be featured on Radio Vision 2000's Internet Web site, receive three hundred U.S. dollars, a twelve-inch color television, two cellular phones, two airline tickets to the historic northern city of Cap Haitien, and two airline tickets for a week's stay in the Dominican Republic. The runners-up will receive consolation prizes from the Alliance Française of Jacmel, which Beaulière is guessing will probably be a volume of poetry written by a local doctor.

Before the event begins, the lights go out. A communal gasp sounds throughout the growing audience. The stars appear larger and even brighter than the fireworks. A silver moon provides enough illumination to allow the spectators to fumble for lighters or flashlights, and for Beaulière to run off and see about a generator.

The lights come back on just as suddenly as they went off.

"We couldn't have that during the carnival weekend," a nearby man shouts triumphantly. "No to blackouts. We refuse blackouts!"

The music comes back on. This time it's Jennifer Lopez's "If You Had My Love," but the lyrics are in Creole. J. Lo in Jacmel? In Creole? It's a soundalike, but youth culture is nothing if not monolithic.

I spot a few young men from a secondary school I had visited earlier in the week, the Lycée Alcibiade Pommayrac. They are mouthing the words to the translated Jennifer Lopez song as they perform elaborate dance steps from the music video. The young men are there to support one of the contestants, a former classmate who is favored for queen.

With the lights back on, the contest begins. Every inch of the club is packed, standing room only. There are only five contestants, as many as there are judges. The first task given to the contestants is to introduce themselves and explain the official origins of the national carnival. The contestants state their names, then take turns giving the same answer, ad-libbing a paragraph from Divers's carnival book:

"Even though it was started in 1992, the national carnival was officially recognized in 1995 in the presence of the country's ministers of culture and tourism, as well as representatives of the press, delegations from all the neighboring regions, and Jacmelians living abroad who had purposely come to support our carnival, their carnival."

The contestants' opening presentations are followed by a theatrical piece about a local man who is pretending to be a *dyaspora,* a Haitian living in the United States. The phony American accent sends the crowd reeling.

The contestants return in new costumes, some in glittery evening gowns, others in denim peasant garb. They walk the perimeter of the stage several times, backs straight, heads held high, like supermodels in a couture show.

"The queen is at the heart of the carnival," Divers had told me earlier. In times past, one queen was chosen by the businessmen and women of the town, who gathered at city hall to make their choice among several exemplary candidates, whom they had been observing all year long. The queen was then given etiquette lessons and speech training to be sure that she represented the cultured ideals of Jacmel. In protest, the people who felt excluded from this selection elected their own queen, La Reine des Brigands, the Queen of the Ruffians. For years, there was fierce competition between the official queen, who was from the upper city, Bel-Air, and the ruffian queen, who was from the lower city.

Both queens were watched very closely.

"When the opposing parties could not question the moral ideals of the other queen," Divers writes in his book, "they examined with a fine-tooth comb her eyes, the thickness of her eyebrows, the size of her lips, her smile, the movement of her hips. It was a blind struggle . . . with enough suspense to break your heart."

These days, however, anyone who can afford a float can elect a queen of his or her own.

The contestants return for another round of questioning. By now the crowd has selected its favorite, the former Lycée Alcybiade Pommayrac student. The final question is, how can Jacmelians assure that the visitors who come for the national carnival have a good time?

"We should surround them with our famous Jacmelian hospitality," the favorite replies, never breaking her perfect smile. She must stop her speech often, as every word she utters is greeted with thundering applause from the Lycée Alcibiade Pommayrac boys. "We should open our doors to those who do not have a place to stay, let them sleep in our beds if the hotels are full."

The crowd roars. Even though the favorite seems a bit startled by the way the sentence has come out.

Sure enough, the former Alcibiade Pommayrac student is the winner. In the rest room, a woman who had her hopes on one of the other contestants complains.

"Like all elections in this country, this one was rigged. That girl wins everything."

The queen elected, the party continues, fireworks bursting with more frequency overhead. There's more of Jennifer Lopez too, this time in English. J. Lo singing heartily and with conviction, "Even if you were broke, my love don't cost a thing."

Seasonal ceremonies not only help to ensure man's survival in the face of natural adversity but express his joy for the successful passing of each phase of the year.

CAROLE BECKWITH
AND ANGELA FISHER,
African Ceremonies

Carnival Day

D AWN UNWINDS SLOWLY on Ti Mouyaj beach, a few miles outside of Jacmel. While the sky brightens from dusk to gray, then various shades of blue, the sea swells up as if to meet the rising sun. A few fishing canoes are anchored along the shore, bobbing on incoming waves. The sea has been exceptionally rough this week, keeping fishermen at bay. So much so that there's no fresh fish to be had in many homes and restaurants in town.

The fishermen know not to venture out. The sea is often like this before *Karèm,* Lent, they say. It becomes merciless and unpredictable, as if to remind humans that their enjoyment and indulgences won't last.

Later that afternoon, five American Airlines employees based in Port-au-Prince will drown on that same beach, not knowing, or neglecting, local legend about the ruggedness of that particular shore at this specific time of year.

෧

THE DAY SEEMS to have begun hours ago for the people walking along the main road leading back to town. Many are wearing their Sunday best, linen suits and flawlessly ironed dresses, as they head to church.

I walk past a roadside cemetery at the foot of a mountain facing the sea. On the gate, carved in metal, are the words REMEMBER THAT YOU ARE DUST AND TO THE DUST YOU SHALL RETURN.

෧

HALF THE PEWS are full for the early mass at Saint Phillipe and Saint Jacques Cathedral, organ music and choir voices echoing down the aisles. The congregrants look beatific as they form a single line to receive Holy Communion. Most are older women who gracefully stroll toward the altar as though they do this every day. The church's stained-glass windows glimmer as the sun moves higher in the sky, the light filtering through the incandescent frames of gospel images.

On the street outside the church, people are going about their daily tasks; a few women and girls carefully balance baskets of produce or buckets of water on their heads. The market, a hub of activity during the week, is a ghost town of bare stands with chairs piled on top of tables. A boy carefully guides his bicycle through a line of cars maneuvering their way down a side street, where an older man is painting the penciled letters on a giant placard that will adorn the float for Jacaya English Institute.

WOMEN CAN MAKE THE DIFFERENCE, the placard reads.

Aside from its cultural aspects, carnival is also a golden opportunity for advertising. The main carnival route, Avenue Baranquilla, is lined with banners from banks and telephone companies wishing everyone a joyous carnival in much smaller lettering than their brand names and logos.

The top-floor stand of the Baranquilla's Café Terrasse is still under construction. However, one of the other prime café viewing locations, Pain K-Dèt, is already open for business, serving breakfast, as are the street vendors who ladle pumpkin soup into plastic bowls at great speed.

Divers and I have chosen Pain K-Dèt for our final pre-carnival rendezvous. He is late; however, he has left word that he will arrive soon.

The clusters of people strolling by Pain K-Dèt are expanding. Car traffic is no longer allowed, except for the police pickups driven by officers with megaphones, who advise motorists to move their parked automobiles.

It is meet-and-greet time for many people wandering up and down the avenue, photographing and videotaping one another. Spontaneous reunions, hugs, and salutations abound. On private balconies overlooking the carnival route, families and friends are already gathering, drinking, and listening to music. A candy and cigarette seller dances as she quickly walks by, shouting *"Sirèt, Sigarèt!"*—a staccato poem calling attention to her merchandise. A woman in a satin cap and gown is trying to catch up with her, as are two men, one with a white cotton panty pulled over his face and the other with a stretched condom around his head.

Divers arrives. He is a bit nervous but definitely excited. Most of the disputes with the bands have been resolved. As for the rest, with the official start of the carnival parade only a few hours away, there is nothing he can do now.

He suggests that we head up to Bel-Air, where a special radio broadcast of older carnival music is being blasted from giant loudspeakers strategically placed in the middle of the square. The Catholic school near city hall is hosting a culinary fair, where foods from different parts of the country are on display: boiled and grilled corn, plantain, millet and rice flour, cane syrup and manioc cakes, fried and stewed chicken, goat, and pork.

"Carnival is a food festival too," one of the vendors of *taso*—fried goat—tells me with a mischievous wink and laugh, "a celebration of *all kinds* of meat."

Indeed the word "carnival" is derived from the Latin *carnelevarium,* meaning the elimination of meat. The Tuesday before Ash Wednesday is known as Mardi Gras, or Fat Tuesday, referring to the day when a corpulent ox would be paraded through city streets.

In his book *Bacchanal!* Peter Mason describes carnival as a time when "Christians were allowed a last chance to eat, drink and be merry, to indulge in the old pagan ways, before the strictures of Lent, when they would be required to give up meat and the sins of the flesh." Carnival is also a way of acknowledging seasonal change, the close of winter and the appearance of spring. Since there are no drastic seasonal variations in Haiti, the carnival can also serve as a marker of these fluctuations, a transitional period between Christmas and Easter.

In rural Haiti, where I would spend the carnival week as a child, this period would sometimes coincide with the planting season, during which a group of men would assemble to work each other's fields. As they raised and lowered their pickaxes and hoes, they would sing to keep the rhythm, calling back and forth to one another like a chain gang gospel choir. The songs were sometimes lively and other times mournful, depending on the pace at which the work needed to be done. As the men worked the fields, the women and children would fetch water and tend to the livestock, all while preparing an elaborate meal to be enjoyed by everyone at the end of the day. Pounding dried corn between mortars and pestles, using graters to scrape the juice out of coconut chunks, the women would sing their own songs, which also varied depending on the intensity of their labor.

Later that day in Jacmel, the carnival parade would feature a group that would include at least three generations of revelers dressed as peasant farmers. The group's leader would be a bare-chested young man with palm trees painted in green dye over his torso and back. He would be accompanied by an older man wearing a denim shirt, a straw hat, and a red scarf around his neck, the old man representing Azaka, the patron god of agriculture, the young man, his joyous servant. Together the two men would perform a variety of peasant dances while waving their rattles like conductors' batons to direct the rest of the ensemble. Most of the group members would have their faces painted in bright red, blue, yellow, and green, as if to form a Technicolor quilt: old men and women in straw hats, young men pushing wheelbarrows full of plants, girls carrying baskets of spices and herbs, one of which looks a lot like the flowers of the crown of the Virgin Mary.

The group's call-and-response hymns would encourage people in the crowd to plant trees while demanding agricultural reform, turning their carnival moment into a jubilant protest. At center stage, however, would be the music. Booming with whistles, drums, graters, conch shells, flutes, and rattles, the songs would sound just as they did during the evening feasts following days of communal work in the fields, inciting weary-bodied dancing late into the night.

At the culinary fair in Bel-Air, I meet a young herbalist who informs me that the flowers of the crown of the Virgin Mary in the cemetery are probably Virginia creepers, belonging to the Vitaceae plant family. The creeper, which also goes by the Creole name of *yanm poul,* chicken liana—perhaps because chickens like to peck at them, he says—can also be used for medicinal purposes, to shrink skin inflammations after a hard day of field labor.

While carnival lasts, there is no other life outside of it. During carnival time, life is subject only to its laws, that is, the laws of its own freedom.

MIKHAIL BAKHTIN,
Rabelais and His World

Life-and-Death Carnival

*I*HAVE BEEN staying in a small second-floor apartment on the Avenue de la Liberté, the starting point of the carnival procession. When I leave Divers, who has to attend to some of his last-minute duties, I return to the front gallery there to watch the carnival groups assemble for the parade.

A few participants and eager spectators begin to gather on the Avenue de la Liberté in midmorning. The scene grows surreal as more and more costumed partakers arrive, with zombies and apes greeting each other, white colonists kissing Arawak Indians, a lion sharing a bottle of juice with a baby alligator, and slaves shaking hands with ghosts and devils. These were the stock ensembles, the ones that consistently went out, with only modest variations, every year.

Without these perennials, a man wearing striped black-and-white overalls and a zebra head tells me, "carnival would not be the same. We are what takes carnival from year to year, so that a child who cannot even walk yet can say he saw the same thing at the carnival as his grand-mother and grandfather did."

"Carnival is a renewal," a woman covered in brown, dried banana leaves chimes in. "Each year while it's taking place, you feel like it is your birthday. You say to yourself, It is happening again. I have lived yet another year to see it."

Carnival, in addition to all else, is a morality play, a chance for some to make a point, pass on a message. The prevailing message this year seems to be about AIDS.

I leave the gallery to trail after a scrawny young man in a dark wig and short black dress with the acronym SIDA (AIDS) painted in white on the back. As he strolls up and down the Avenue de la Liberté, he raises the dress to show white panties with red blotches on them. When he stops to growl at passersby, he bares his teeth, which are covered in black ink. A solo act, this man will draw laughter as well as moans during the carnival parade.

"That's SIDA," people will point and say.

As he'll walk to the officials' stand, which will include the many carnival queens, several local dignitaries, and the U.S. ambassador, the carnival narrator and ritual ring-mistress, Michaelle Craan, will wipe her honey-colored face with her handkerchief, shift her microphone from one hand to the other, and moan before presenting him to the crowd.

"My friends," she will declare in a dramatic voice, "the carnival of Jacmel consists of many things." Then, signaling for the man to move closer, she'll say, "This person represents AIDS, my friends. AIDS, show them how ugly you are. Show them how destructive you can be. Show them how you can kill people."

The man will pout his brightly painted red lips and blow a menacing kiss at the crowd. He'll grit his black teeth, growl, and try to make a muscle bulge in his bony arm as the crowd looks on.

This man will not be the only carnival participant with an AIDS message. A large group of young people from a local health organization, some wearing simple masks with their jeans and T-shirts, others wearing no masks at all, will stroll through the crowd handing out condoms, while two of them carry a banner that reads LET'S BREAK THE SILENCE ABOUT AIDS.

A smaller group will carry a sign that reads CARNIVAL IS PLEASURE FOR A FEW DAYS—WITH A CONDOM, THE PLEASURE WILL LAST FOREVER. The symbol for AIDS in this crew is a ghost with a rope tied around his waist. Each time the ghost attempts to get near a reveler, the young man holding the rope forcefully reigns him in. In this group, AIDS is also represented as skeletons carrying hammers and crosses, tapping them together to sound a death knell.

AIDS is a painfully complicated issue for us Haitians; even though we represented only 6 percent of the patients when it first surfaced, in the late 1970s and early 1980s, we were branded as the originators of the disease. In his book *AIDS and Accusation: Haiti and the Geography of Blame,* the physician Paul Farmer, who has worked in Haiti for many years, observed that "popular acceptance of the scientific community's allegation that AIDS came from Haiti was rapid and complete." Along with chronic political unrest, many blame this belief for the complete demise of the pre-1980s tourism boom, which had bought, among others, Miles Davis, Errol Flynn, Ava Gardner, Irving Berlin, and Mick Jagger to the island. Even as later scientific findings revealed that Haitians were no more likely than anyone else involved in high-risk behavior to acquire AIDS, the stigma remained, most recently manifesting itself in the 1998 feature film based on the Terry McMillan novel *How Stella Got Her Groove Back*. The main character, played by Angela Bassett, upon returning from a vacation in Jamaica is told by one of her sisters, "I hope you used a condom, because you know those people have a history of AIDS." In response, another sister, a healthcare professional, proclaims, "That's Haiti, Miss Manners."

Haitians have had the dual task of dealing with worldwide finger-pointing about AIDS while tackling its alarming expansion at home. And at carnival, the man in the black dress, in his grotesque personification of AIDS, is saying to everyone that yes, it does exist here; but the young people with the banners are also saying that it is not ours alone.

THE OFFICIAL PARADE starts shortly after noon with a menagerie of animals, giant papier-mâché masks topping multicolored costumes representing each species in vibrant

detail: lions, alligators, zebras, apes, giraffes, frogs, croco-
diles, flamingos, parrots, horses, rhinoceroses, elephants,
snakes, dragons, dinosaurs, rabbits, even yellow-eyed mice
that look like laboratory mutants.

As I follow the mask menagerie down the Avenue de
la Liberté toward the Baranquilla, I think of the very first
masks worn by our hunter-gatherer ancestors: the hol-
lowed heads of slain animals.

Animal masks "were among the first and most logical
images and disguises for man, whose major immediate
experiences were in the animal world," the theater historian Walter Sorell writes in *The Other Face: The Mask in
the Arts*. "The mask was undoubtedly preceded by the
painting of the body, the first realization of man's sense of
decoration."

This sense of decoration is extravagantly exaggerated
in Jacmel's bright papier-mâché animals, who are actually
ambulant sculptures with a range of facial casts from the
watchful and fierce expressions of the adult animals to the
innocent miens of their offspring. In many ways strolling
among them is like walking through a circus, or watching
a group pantomime up close, as the adults and children
beneath the costumes try their best to mimic the gait and
carriage of each animal, sometimes interacting with one
another but mostly engaging the crowd by edging toward
them to allow for a better look.

Jacmel's carnival is best known for these papier-mâché
masks. Whether they are carved to look like animals,
world figures, or the local politician of the day, they are

what people remember most from the parade. Jacmelians like to brag that these masks would stand out in any carnival, even in the richest countries in the world. And they are right. Both playful and ceremonial, these masks seemed to have jumped out of Haitian paintings, which often depict an older, wilder Haiti, with lush forests and jungles sheltering indigenous animals as well as species that have never been seen on the island, all of it forming a living fable, a chimerical Noah's Ark, a symbolic journey between the present and a very distant past.

Of the animal figures in the carnival, the most popular seems to be the Mathurin, for it appears in various forms in several groups. A batlike monster with horns, it stops every now and then to clack its large wooden wings to frighten anyone close by. Legend has it that this costume takes its name from its designer, a young Jacmelian named Mathurin Gousse; when he first appeared in it at a costume ball he was nearly shot to death by a local policeman, who believed he was looking at a real devil.

The largest gathering of Mathurins can be seen around a man dressed as the dragon-slayer archangel, Saint Michel. Simulating a battle between good and evil, the Mathurins smack their wings at Saint Michel and his entourage of child angels, while Saint Michel fights back with a golden sword.

The Protestant Church, which in recent years has gained a very strong hold on predominantly Catholic Haiti, is also represented in the carnival, by a group of men, women, and children in white belting out religious songs. They too are provoked by the Mathurins, which they ignore completely as they march on.

Trailing the Mathurins is an enigmatic carnival figure called the *Juif Errant,* or the Wandering Jew. He sports a long snow-white beard with matching hair and mustache; if not for the tattered old jacket, the soiled white apron, and the ballooned pants, the *Juif Errant* could easily be mistaken for Santa Claus.

Some Haitians, commenting on widespread migration from Haiti due to political prosecution and economic instability, compare their plight to that of the Wandering Jew and other nomadic figures.

Common lore has it that the carnival figure is a representation of an innkeeper who refused to let Jesus rest on his front steps as Jesus was carrying his cross up Mount Calvary. For this, the innkeeper was cursed with immortality and condemned to wander the earth until Christ's Second Coming.

In her book *Rara! Vodou, Power, and Performance in Haiti and Its Diaspora,* anthropologist Elizabeth McCalister argues that the *Juif Errant*'s presence in the carnival "is not a clear-cut case of anti-Judaism (or anti-Semitism). . . . 'The Jews' were marked as the original 'Other' of Europe, the very first object of projection, marginalization, and demonization of Christendom. Europe's demonization of the Jews became a mythological blueprint for the encounter with Native peoples and Africans in the Americas."

As if to emphasize the ambiguity of this relationship, the *Juif Errant* on the parade route is accompanied by two men dressed in army uniforms, guards who could either be protecting him or keeping him under arrest.

THE PARADE IS in full force by midafternoon. I move along with the different groups filing down the Baranquilla: the Arawaks, the slaves and colonists, the zombies and *chaloskas,* the ghosts, the AIDS educators, and the peasant farmers. I check that the mule with the tennis shoes is there, along with the single king at carnival, a handsome young man riding a dark brown horse through the crowd while wearing a white gold-trimmed robe and a gold paper crown on his head. Perhaps aware of the Greco-Roman myth of the carnival king as a defiant exile from Mount Olympus, a woman calls out that the king is actually a *dyaspora,* a Haitian from abroad, who is not on the official parade roster.

The same woman who is heckling the king blows her whistle and hands me a stick to whack the cowhide-covered Yawe nearby, but I pass, fearing that I might hurt the person underneath. Instead, I head toward a group of men in pastel-colored suits and coattails, men representing the old inn owners of what has always been a tourist-conscious city. At the turn of the twentieth century, a ship used to sail from here to Long Island, New York. The British Royal Mail stopped here. And now a new port is being built with a reception area to receive cruise ships. Once again the innkeepers could become the premiere citizens of the town.

Moving on to Max Power's string of world figures, I shake hands with Gandhi and Nelson Mandela and pose for a picture with Che Guevara. The only group I am afraid to get too close to is a band of bare-chested horned and hooded men whose bodies are covered with sugar-cane syrup mixed with soot and powdered carbon. Baptized *lanceurs de cordes,* or rope launchers, these men gather closely together behind a rope and then launch into a fast run, all the while trying to rub the sticky ash on their bodies on revelers.

Reminiscent of the predawn *J'Ouvert* or "Dirty Mas" processions on neighborhood islands, these purposefully darkened Dionysuses seem to be playing a game of hide-and-seek with both the children and the adult revelers, who flee from them or cling to one another in order to avoid getting soiled. I become breathless after a few runs, not having trained myself like the *lanceurs,* who perform push-ups between launches.

I move toward a smaller assembly around the *krapo,* or frog, a small boy in a green leotard whose belly and behind are stuffed with rags. He is dancing on two wooden poles, gyrating his tiny hips to the rhythm of a frenzied drumbeat while performing a high-wire act on the beams. According to Divers, the *krapo* act was started by young people who wanted more than anything to make revelers laugh. With each exaggerated movement of his tiny body, the *krapo* arouses belly laughs. Encouraged by the response, the boy tries even harder, rotating his arms and legs in opposite directions while the plank holders sing, "A frog has no ass, how is it that he is able to dance?"

In midafternoon, most of the onlookers leave the sidelines and join the parade. I make my way up to the official viewing stand, where each act stops to be introduced to the queens, politicians, and dignitaries. As I arrive, the American ambassador is taking a brief spin with the carnival narrator and ritual ringmistress, Michaelle Craan. They are dancing together to a vigorous carnival song blaring from a nearby loudspeaker. Like many carnival songs, this one is a protest hymn, a musical parabasis.

"We are selling the country in U.S. dollars," goes the chorus.

The music is thumping so loudly that neither Craan nor the U.S. ambassador seem to be aware of the lyrics.

The different carnival queens, who fill up most of the front row, are rocking in their seats, bobbing their heads even after the song has ended.

By this time, the large floats, equipped with their own live bands or recorded music, are beginning to surface, starting with the one from Jacaya English Institute, whose queen rotates her hips around a pole as she waves a white lace hanky at the crowd.

Max Power makes its second appearance with two large floats, one a replica of a United States Coast Guard cutter outfitted with a mast, watchtower, direction find-ers, and antennas. On the main deck are men dressed as Coast Guard officers, their oversized masks dwarfing the rest of their bodies. The Coast Guard faces are multi-cultural, with black, white, and brown skin tones. Each "guard," a patroller of international waters, is holding a papier-mâché gun as he turns his masked head from side to side, as though on high alert.

Behind the make-believe Coast Guard cutter is a small wooden boat with refugees packed shoulder to shoulder on the decks. There are cardboard cutouts of sharks slithering back and forth on the side of the boat, menacing its frightened passengers. The forward movement of densely packed revelers on foot effortlessly mime the waves on the high seas.

In front of the viewing stand, the two vessels come together and the Coast Guard officers board the smaller boat, forcing a few of the refugees to jump overboard, into the crowd. Deep in the middle of the crowd, I have lost sight of the U.S. ambassador. I can't help but wonder what he is thinking, or even if he is still on the viewing stand.

Max Power is acting out a crisis that many Haitians know only too well: U.S. Coast Guard officers intercepting refugees at sea. According to Amnesty International, in 1991, after the coup that unseated President Aristide during his first term, thirty-eight thousand Haitians took to the high seas, crossing five hundred miles of rough waters to Miami. Of those, less than 5 percent received asylum and the rest were repatriated. Between that time and now, thousands have perished at sea, their boats sinking or simply disappearing somewhere between Haiti and Miami.

The carnivalesque disaster, wrote Bakhtin, frees us from fear of an actual tragedy, turning it into a "sequence of gay transformations and renewals." I see the Max Power float as renewed political protest but also as a cautionary tale, as well as a tribute to those who have perished at sea while dreaming of a better life.

Max Power is an enormous hit, its only close competitor being a giant butterfly. A marvel of gold and green cardboard and papier-mâché, it is a visual as well as mechanical wonder. It is so tall that the electric cables along the parade route must be raised to allow it to pass. After the boat-people re-creation, the butterfly seems to be a symbol of hope, a sign that beauty can follow tragedy, that splendor can follow pain.

After Max Power and the butterfly, the procession part of the parade gives way to full, unconstrained dancing. Divers was right; there are thousands of people competing for space on the Baranquilla and the surrounding streets.

I become part of the massive flock following Relax Band's bright orange float, feeling both encased and embraced by the slow-moving crowd. Everyone is jumping up and down, hands up in the air as if to touch discernible spirits dancing above our heads.

According to Bakhtin, one of the oldest descriptions of carnival is of a priest's mystic vision of hell. In this vision the priest saw an army of people walking toward him on a deserted street "wearing the skins of wild beasts." The army was followed by men carrying coffins and baskets. "Next came a great number of women on horseback," he wrote. "Their saddles were studded with red-hot nails, onto which they fell as they rode. Last came the clergy and soldiers enveloped in flames. All these marchers were souls of dead sinners . . . migrants from purgatory expatiating their sins."

I can no longer resist the contagious revelry. I am one of those women now, loving and fearing the sensation of red-hot nails pricking me all over, and all I can do is dance and dance for relief from their sting. I am among the clergy and soldiers in flames. I am one of those marchers and migrants, back from the purgatory of exile, expatiating sins of coldness and distance.

At last, my body is a tiny fragment of a much larger being. I am part of a group possession, a massive stream of joy. I feel like I am twirling around a maypole, and going much too fast, and I cannot stop. My head is spinning, but I don't care. There is nothing that seems to matter as much as following the curve of the other bodies pressed against mine. In that brief space and time, the carnival offers all the paradoxical elements I am craving: anonymity, jubilant community, and belonging.

I now wish that I had chosen a more ritually spectacular costume for my carnival day than my T-shirt, jeans, and straw hat. During one of my leaps upward with the crowd, my straw hat slips off my head, sliding down the back of my neck. There is not enough room for me to turn back and look for it. I am not even sure it fell to the ground. It may have simply slipped onto another head.

All of a sudden, the sky darkens and it begins to rain. It's been years now since I have been out in the rain in Haiti. When I was a girl, whenever it rained, my cousins and I—whether we were in the mountains or the city—would go out and get wet. Sometimes we would soap ourselves up for an outdoor shower. Other times it was simply for the pleasure of feeling raindrops tapping against our skin.

The rain lasts only a few minutes, but it thins out the crowd. I take advantage of this to abandon Relax Band for a few smaller groups, the *bann apye* (bands on foot) with no floats or speakers, just homemade, handheld instruments, whistles and graters and bamboo flutes.

By now it is almost dark. After hours on my feet, I decide to take a rest. I snake my way through the crowd and head back to Café Terrasse, where Rodney and a group of his friends have gathered to watch the carnival from a second-floor stand.

One of Jacmel's two major musical groups, Les Invincibles, makes its appearance. Fireworks explode overhead to greet the Invisibles' float.

"We are back on the scene," they sing, the speakers blasting the lead singer's rasping voice along with echoes of screeching guitars, humming keyboards, and buzzing drum machine.

Just my luck, Café Terrasse is an Invincibles sponsor, so the group parks itself in front of the café, singing for the Terrasse guests.

Les Invincibles' strength seems to be its deep connection with the crowd, a sense of shared history demonstrated by the crowd's ability to sing the choruses of its audience-inclusive lyrics even before the singer gets to them.

"Here's your band, your favorite band," the lead singer ad-libs. "We're back on the scene *for you.*"

Once the Terrasse performance has ended, the crowd gathers again in full force, pushing the Invincibles float forward, it seems, on its energy alone, making requests from the Invincibles' repertoire, which the group obliges with abandon.

It is said that the musical groups stop playing only when the flatbed trucks run out of gas or when the generators that power their electrical instruments run out of fuel. The Invincibles' lead singer promises the crowd that the band has enough fuel to go on all night.

Les Invincibles moves on from the café, its ambulant audience trailing it, down the Baranquilla. I head back to the Avenue de la Liberté to the house where I am staying. There, Les Invincibles' fierce competitor, Jouvenceaux, the group that had been involved in the fire, is gearing up to head out, with an enthusiastic assembly of loyal followers behind it.

The woman who lives downstairs from the apartment where I am staying, Edline, spots me on the street and calls me over. A demure housekeeper in her forties, she asks if I can look after her four-year-old goddaughter, Faby, while she checks out Jouvenceaux. She has been inside all day, and has not had a chance to see any of the carnival, she says. Baby-sitting Faby could mean my being grounded, perhaps for the rest of the evening, but the look of urgent anticipation on Edline's face forces me to say yes. Faby is heartbroken, however, that she is not accompanying her godmother and begins to cry as Edline skips out into the night without her.

Developing second thoughts about agreeing to baby-sit, I nevertheless tell Faby, and perhaps myself, that we can sit on the house's front gallery and watch another kind of carnival: the carnival of mothers and fathers coming out to look for their children who have not yet come home, the carnival of friends reuniting after a day of being in different extensions of the crowd, the carnival of people walking home wearing only part of their costumes.

Faby is not buying this, but she stops crying and resigns herself to the fact that she will not be going to carnival that night.

Faby and I sit on the front gallery for a while and watch another stream of revelers heading out to join either Les Invincibles or Jouvenceaux further along their route. Rodney surfaces and we take Faby with us for a meal in a restaurant down the block. In the restaurant, we spot some musicians from Tabou Combo, an internationally known musical group, who have come out to check out carnival. The waitress gives them all her attention, and by the time our fried plantains arrive, Faby has fallen asleep in my arms.

As Rodney and I eat, we can hear music from several directions, old Spanish boleros over the restaurant's loudspeakers, makeshift *bann a pye* just venturing out into the street, young people on a front gallery listening to Haitian-flavored hip-hop on a boom box, and, in the distance, the cacophony of Invincibles and Jouvenceaux heading for the inevitable musical showdown at some crossroads.

By the time we return to the house, Faby's godmother is back.

Did she have a good time, I ask.

She nods with a big smile on her face.

Surrendering a sleeping and perhaps dreaming Faby, I give up the idea of heading out into the night in search of further carnival encounters. In my mind is still some lingering apprehension that in the night, I might finally face the type of carnival that I had been warned against by my uncle, the type of carnival that renders one mute and deaf, the carnival of beatings and stabbings, of being squeezed like a sponge by some lusty stranger when I have so little energy to resist.

Back in my room, as I prepare for bed, I think of the image of the carnival that I'd had as a girl as one big raucous party, which would do me more harm than good. I marveled at how it had never occurred to me, even as a child, that I was already part of the carnival, that it was always all around me. Like Camille Saint-Saëns, who composed the suite *Carnival of the Animals* because he had not been allowed to go to carnival, I had made this singular carnival day my own. What I hadn't realized, however, is that I'd had days like this before, even if in fragments and pieces. The carnivals I had spent in the mountains were not all that different from the one I had seen today. Nor was the one I had glimpsed in segments from the front steps of my uncle's house in Port-au-Prince. Those too were celebrations of life, community, and belonging, explosions of rapture and beauty in a country that is not supposed to have any joy.

I can still hear music blasting from many directions as I slip into bed. As I drift off to sleep, I wish that I could dream young Faby's dreams, visit the carnival in her head, watch the fanciful scraps from her brief exposure to the day, meld into a carnival uniquely her own.

I felt privileged that I'd had a taste of both carnivals: the carnival of my imagination and the one I'd been part of today, which had been like a communal dream, a public wonderland shared by thousands of others.

A FEW HOURS later, at three in the morning, I am startled awake by a song screeching to a sudden halt. There is dead silence and then a voice shouts into a loudspeaker. It sounds like the raspy voice of the Invincibles' lead singer, a bit lower and deeper now after a whole afternoon and evening of constant singing.

"We have no more gas," he declares. "The party is over."

Whether I am actually hearing his voice or imagining it, I am not sure. But just as suddenly, it is silent again, the carnival giving back to the night its habitual cloak of calm and tranquillity.

I go back to sleep, returning to my own dreams, which are less like dreams now and more like recollections, a series of mental slides of all that I have seen and experienced on what is already a day away.

After the dance, the drum is heavy.

HAITIAN PROVERB

The Day After

*J*ACMEL IS BACK to its calm and slow-paced rhythm the next morning. I meet Divers at the square for one last chat. We are both bleary-eyed but renewed. Divers is relieved and satisfied. The national carnival was a success, he says. Few people have complained. He's checked with the hospitals and the police. There were some scuffles. A handful of revelers were wounded, but no one was gravely hurt.

"So is the drum heavy today?" I ask him.

"Not so bad," he says.

It may have been heavier for him before.

After I say good-bye to Divers, Rodney and I meet for lunch at a small restaurant in Bel-Air. On one of the cafeteria-length tables is a television, which is replaying scenes from carnival the day before.

The other customers comment as they watch and eat. They praise the masks, the costumes, and the music. There is none of the harsh criticism that Divers had feared.

Halfway through the meal, I spot myself briefly on the television screen. I am inside one of those small groups with handheld instruments, a *bann a pye,* and we are singing a popular song about someone who loses a hat on a road between the town and the valley of Jacmel.

"I leave the town of Jacmel," the song begins, "to go to the valley. While arriving at Bainet Crossroads, my Panama hat fell down. My Panama hat fell down. My Panama hat fell down. Those who come behind me, pick it up for me."

This had been one of my favorite songs as a child, even before I had been to Jacmel. Seeing myself singing it now on that television screen, my head cocked back, my arms draped around people I didn't even know, I had a strange feeling of detachment. Was that really me? So unencumbered, so lively, so free.

So it did happen after all. I had really been there. Even as others had been putting on their masks, just for one afternoon, I had allowed myself to remove my own.

Acknowledgments

I am extremely grateful to Michelet Divers, Rodney Saint-Eloi, Consuela and Ronald Mews, Edline Prudent, Fedo Boyer, Lewis Kornhauser, Axelle Liautaud, Gerald Borne and the teachers and students of Lycée Alcibiade Pommayrac, Paskal Flaubass, Paula Hyppolite, Papayo, Kathy Dorce, Emile Michel and his family, and Dr. Georges Greffin for all their help, hospitality, and suggestions. *Mèsi anpil! Anpil!*

About the Author

EDWIGE DANTICAT is the author of *Breath, Eyes, Memory; Krik? Krak!; The Farming of Bones;* and *Behind the Mountains,* a young adult novel. She is also the editor of *The Butterfly's Way: Voices from the Haitian Dyaspora in the United States* as well as *The Beacon Best of 2000: Great Writing by Women and Men of All Colors and Cultures.*

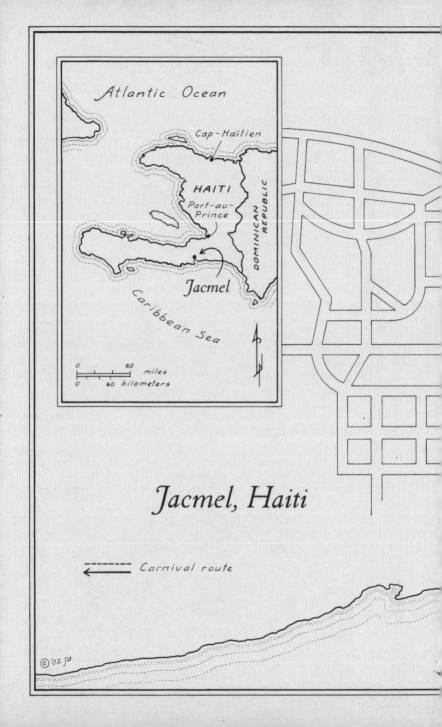

Atlantic Ocean

Cap-Haïtien

HAITI

Port-au-
Prince

DOMINICAN REPUBLIC

Jacmel

Caribbean Sea

0   60 miles
0   60 kilometers

N

Jacmel, Haiti

- - - - - - - → Carnival route

© '02 Ja